THE ULTIMATE BABYSITTING COURSE

COURSE MANUAL

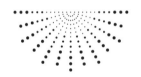

L.A. HOEKSTRA

THE ULTIMATE BABYSITTING COURSE
Course Manual

L.A. HOEKSTRA

LEGAL LIABILITY DISCLAIMER

The material provided in the "The Babysitter Club" training course and manual is intended for educational purposes only.

Topics include:

- The roles and responsibilities of babysitters
- The benefits of being a babysitter
- The benefits of being a licensed babysitter
- How to care for infants, toddlers, preschool, and school-aged children
- How to keep safe and solve problems
- What to do in emergency situations

A certificate of course completion and licence are given upon course completion, which signifies that the individual completed the course. This certificate in no way denotes the level of competence.

In preparation for this course, every effort has been made to offer the most current, correct, and up-to-date information as possible.

In no event shall the course provider be held liable, nor shall any course instructors or any of their subsidiaries be held liable to any entity for any direct, indirect, special, consequential, or other damages related to the use of or inability to use the course content.

MISSION STATEMENT

THE ULTIMATE BABYSITTING COURSE

To teach pre-teens and teenagers leadership and safety skills to confidently care for babies to school-aged children in a professional and respectful positive environment with care, compassion and putting the children's needs and safety at the highest priority.

Kids are worth it!

Listen to the Ultimate Babysitting Course Manual
"FREE on Audible"
with a 30-day trial!
Click Here!

https://www.audible.com/pd/B08FRB25S1/?source_code=AUDFPWS0223189MWT-BK-ACX0-210470&ref=acx_bty_BK_ACX0_210470_rh_us

INTRODUCTION

Welcome to The Ultimate Babysitting Course! I'm so happy you have taken the time to learn, in a fun atmosphere, how to become an excellent babysitter! The material contained in this guide was developed from the list resources listed in references.

People often ask whether a babysitter is the same as a nanny. The definitive answer is no. A babysitter takes over child care duties temporarily to free the child's primary caregiver for a couple of hours. Likewise, a nanny is tasked with the responsibility of caring for a child full time and overseeing their schedule. Some nannies live with the family and are typically trained professionals specializing in childcare. Babysitters are most often people in the parents' support system that pitch in to help. However, to become an effective babysitter in your community, you should take a course to help you be effective.

That is the primary reason we have created this book for you. It is a course that will help you become the best babysitter you can be for the child you are caring for.

In this course, you will learn:

- The qualities of an excellent babysitter
- The benefits of becoming a licensed babysitter
- How to find a babysitting job, write a basic resume, and questions to ask parents
- How to care for infants, toddlers, preschool, and school-aged children
- How to keep yourself and the children in your care safe and solve problems
- What to do when minor accidents and emergency situations occur
- A look inside your Ultimate Babysitting Kit
- Question and answer time
- A test and award ceremony

Babysitting is fun and rewarding. It's an important job with lots of responsibility.

Let's get started.

THE QUALITIES OF AN EXCELLENT BABYSITTER

An excellent babysitter must love kids and have strong values and an honest moral compass, knowing and understanding right from wrong. The truth is that not everyone makes a good babysitter, and it is important to evaluate whether you are a good fit for child care specialization or not. The good news is that, if you are passionate about following this career path, you can develop certain qualities in yourself. Some qualities you can grow and develop include:

Time Management

It is crucial to learn to arrange your time so you are at the kid's home on time. This not only speaks for how seriously you take the job, but it also shows how much you value the time you spend with the kids. Respecting everyone else's time ensures they respect yours as well.

Patience

We all need to grow in our patience, some more than others, and especially where kids are involved. There are plenty of self help books that will help you master the art of patience. When you approach learning patience, think of it as a holistic lesson that benefits you beyond your work environment. Patience is an important ingredient in getting kids to trust you.

Creativity

Children respond to a creative environment in which they can let their imagination flow. Along with this, parents love a creative individual spending time with their kids. This is because they know that the time you spend together will be beneficial to their little one. Learn some creative games and activities that will keep the child both entertained and educated at the same time.

Certification

Certification is important to let the parents know that you are skilled at caring for their child. Start with the most basic certification, like CPR or first aid certifications, which you can expand on as you grow in your career. Parents will want to know that you can handle a medical emergency when they are not around.

Also, consider the following:

- An excellent babysitter is happy, vibrant, courageous, and optimistic!
- Strive to be the very best version of yourself!
- To do this, you should be groomed, kind, rested, and hydrated.

Here are seven traits that many parents often look for in an excellent babysitter:

1. **Responsible**—a reliable babysitter lets the parents know that they can depend on you to care for their children.
2. **Trustworthy**—being trustworthy is perhaps one of the most valuable assets of an excellent babysitter!

Parents want to trust that you will follow their rules, keep the children safe, and have fun at the same time.

3. **Playful**—parents and their children will want a lighthearted, fun, and playful babysitter with an optimistic personality.

4. **Flexible**—parents appreciate a babysitter who can be flexible. Sometimes, their plans may change or they find themselves running late.

5. **Confident**—parents want to trust that you can be confident enough to follow their schedule, and enforce their rules. You should be gentle and kind, and at the same time make it clear to the children that you are in charge.

6. **Patient**—patience is an important virtue for a babysitter to have. Children can sometimes be demanding and uncooperative while trying to bend the rules. Having a patient attitude will make the babysitting job much smoother for everyone.

7. **Skilled**—parents agree across the board that they would hire a skilled and licensed babysitter with experience over someone who has never taken a course or babysat before.

Taking the ultimate babysitting course is a step in the right direction to becoming an excellent and confident babysitter.

Can you list some traits that you have that would make you an excellent babysitter?

1. _____
2. _____
3. _____
4. _____
5. _____
6. _____
7. _____
8. _____
9. _____
10. _____

BENEFITS OF BEING A LICENSED BABYSITTER:

A licensed babysitter is an individual who has received specialized training in babysitting responsibilities, which prepares them to provide excellent childcare. The Ultimate Babysitting Course teaches safety skills that will help you make good decisions when babysitting, along with life skills that will help you in your life, beyond babysitting.

A licensed babysitter will understand:

- responsibility
- problem-solving
- decision making
- leadership
- how to care for infants to school-aged children, and keep them happy and safe

- what to do in an emergency situation

Having your "ultimate" babysitting license is a way to gain experience while earning some money too!

HOW TO FIND A BABYSITTING JOB

Once you've completed the Ultimate Babysitting Course, the next step would be to find a babysitting job.

The best way is to spread the word to your family and friends. Let them know that you have completed the ultimate babysitting course and that you are eager to start babysitting.

For safety reasons, it is best to avoid advertising your services to strangers. Stick close to home and try to limit your neighbours, family, and friends that you know. However, there are other ways to find good babysitting jobs.

ADDITIONAL WAYS TO FIND BABYSITTING JOBS

The Homeowners Association Newsletter

If you live in a neighborhood where the local homeowner's association prints newsletters of jobs in the community, this could be a goldmine. Alternatively, you can also advertise your services to people in the neighborhood. There may be at a small fee, but it will be well worth it.

Bulletin boards

Community centers, coffee shops, and even the library can be great places to put up posters of your services. You may also find parents who are looking for a babysitter on the posters put up there.

Mom groups

Mom groups at the local playgroup will definitely have someone looking to hire your services. Also, any local religious centers, spas. and day care centers can be excellent hunting grounds for babysitting jobs.

Job boards

There are also some safe babysitting job boards online. Babysitting websites are relatively safe because you can have a sit down with the parents and "interview" them before accepting the job. The contract drawn up between the parents and yourself should leave wiggle room for you to exit it without any harsh financial implications. This is your safe exit in case you feel exploited or in any type of danger.

RESUME BASICS

The purpose of a resume is to provide a summary of your contact information, education, skills, experience, accomplishments, and references. Having good references will also triple your chances of landing that babysitting job!

You have to ask permission to use someone as a reference. Call them before you pass out your resume to let them know that they have been added as one of your references and that they might receive a phone call from your potential employer!

There are several online courses and programs that you can use to create a resume. First-time babysitters will benefit from online samples of resumes that have been used by other babysitters. You can find free tools online to help you with this task, such as Canva, VisualCV, and resume.com.

Here is a sample of a basic resume for you to use as a guideline.

(Sample)

Brooke Johnson

123-456-789

777 7th Avenue West Owen Sound, ON N4K 6Y9
brookexjohnson@hotmail.com

Objective

Seeking a part-time babysitting job while attending school full time.

Highlights of Skills

- Positive and enthusiastic personality
- Organized and a good team player

Employment Experience

Sun Times, Owen Sound, ON — 2017 - current

Paper Route Carrier

- Deliver papers to 21 customers and flyers to 55 customers

Owen Sound Attack Hockey, Owen Sound, ON — 2018 - current

Media Room Advisor (Attack Games)

- Greet and sign-in hockey scouts, and media staff
- Serve beverages/food to approximately 60 visitors

BBQ Catering Server (yearly fund-raiser)

- Serve food to players, staff, fans, and volunteers
- Replenish buffer
- Set-up / tear down and wipe down tables
- Clean-up area

Private Employers (seven different families), Owen Sound, ON 2017 - current

Babysitter—responsible for up to 3 children (2 - 5 years of age)

Dog Walker

Education

Currently enrolled in Grade 8 at Hillcrest Elementary School — Owen Sound, ON

Interests/Activities/Community Work

- Canoeing, Kayaking, Fishing, Skiing, Dance
- Volunteer at Calvary Missionary Church Nursery (6 mos. - 2 years of age)
- Volunteer at Selah Camp kitchen helper
- Alliance Church Youth Group member

References available upon request

QUESTIONS TO ASK IN A TELEPHONE INTERVIEW

Parents will typically want to know whom they are leaving their precious little one with. They are concerned about several things, including how the child will react to you, and also how good a fit you are for their child's personality.

Parents want to know that you will not deviate from the parenting technique they have in place because doing so could potentially disrupt the baby's routine.

The various questions that could come from the parents can cause you to concentrate on alleviating their fears. After you have answered all these questions, you will need to turn the conversation back to focus on the baby. That is why we recommend the below approach.

When a parent calls you to babysit, you should first ask them from where they got your name and number. This will let you know what they expect from you in terms of the rate. Once that is out of the way, here is a list of questions you should ask during a telephone interview.

1. What is(/are) your name(s)?

_____

2. What is your address?

_____

3. The date and time of the job

_____

4. Expected hours: from _____

to _____

5. How many children will I be babysitting?

_____

6. Names and ages of the kids

1. Name: _____ Age:_____

2. Name: _____ Age:_____

3. Name: _____ Age:_____

4. Name: _____ Age:_____

7. Will you pick me up and drive me home? _____

8. Do you have any pets? _____

9. Pets' names

_____

10. Do any of the children have special needs or concerns, like allergies?

_____

11. Do you have a pool or hot tub?

_____

(Let the parents know if you are uncomfortable with taking the kids swimming)

12. What is the rate of pay per hour? $ _____

13. May I come 30 minutes before or earlier to prepare myself? ____

14. Can you fill out my safety information sheet before you leave? ____

It's always important to discuss the details of each babysitting job with your own parents before you accept a babysitting job. Some questions you can discuss with parents before taking a babysitting job include:

Do the kids take any medication and if so, how is it administered?

Are there any legal issues surrounding the child?

Who is allowed near the child and who isn't?

Are there rules about screen time?

Can I take photos with your child?

RESPONSIBILITIES AND EXPECTATIONS

Every family will be a little bit different. It is important to get to know each family and their expectations and rules. There are several types of families that will employ your services:

The Nuclear Family

This family consists of a mom, dad, and child or children. Babysitting for this type of family means you are caring for the children in their family home. This may be the typical babysitting gig that many babysitters are used to or will be initially expecting.

In this type of family, there may also be scenarios that include biological or adopted parents and their children, a single parent household with a child involved, or a family child care home. In the latter, there would be a small group of children living with one or two caregivers. This type of home is known as a certified child care home.

Child care centers

You can be a babysitter at the local child care center. These centers have children categorized by age, and they are typically operated in commercial buildings. There is usually a director running the facility, and you can work as one of the staff members.

Preschool programs

These programs are available for kids between the ages of 3-5 years. You will be supervised by the people running the program, depending on where it is located. Preschool programs can be run by the school administration, local church, or volunteers from the local community center.

It is important to fill out the emergency information safety sheet with the parents before they leave. There is a pad included in your Ultimate Babysitting Kit.

School age program

These are programs offering child care services before and after school hours. School-age programs can also run into the holidays and school breaks.

In all the above cases, you will need to have an emergency contact information sheet to help you in times of crisis. Here is what it looks like.

EMERGENCY CONTACT INFORMATION SHEET

Date: _____

For emergencies dial 911

Home address: _____

_____

_____

_____

_____

_____

_____

_____

_____

Phone number: _____

Emergency	Number	Name
POISON CONTROL CENTRE	1-800-222-1222	
TELEHEALTH ONTARIO		
HOSPITAL		
DOCTOR		
DENTIST		
MISCELLANEOUS		

Health Card numbers:

Name _____

Card Number _____

Name _____

Card Number _____

Name _____

Card Number _____

Name _____

Card Number _____

Name _____

Card Number _____

Parents' names:

_____

_____

Mom cell phone: _____

Dad cell phone: _____

Kids' names:

1. _____

2. _____

3. _____

4. _____

Emergency contact:

1) _____

2) _____

Comments/concerns:

———————————————

———————————————

———————————————

———————————————

———————————————

———————————————

———————————————

———————————————

———————————————

PARENT QUESTIONNAIRE

Ask your parents Check box when they agree.

1. Their contact information while away (place they intend to be).
2. Do any of the children have special needs, like allergies? ____
3. Transportation: how will I get to and from your place?
4. What is the rate of pay?
5. Do you expect any extra household chores?
6. Do you have a pet or pets? Names

   _____

7. May I have a friend over?
8. When can I use my cellphone to text? Can I use your WiFi?

9. May I do homework?
10. May I come thirty minutes early to get settled?
11. Special rules, routines, I need to know.

(special concerns and notes follow)

NOTES

RULES OF THE HOUSE:

_____

_____

_____

_____

_____

_____

_____

_____

_____

SAFETY CHECKLIST

- First aid kit
- Telephone

ROUTINES

- Bedtime routine

_____

_____

_____

_____

_____

_____

_____

- Meal/snack time routine

_____

_____

_____

_____

_____

_____

_____

_____

SAFETY TIPS:

_____

_____

_____

_____

_____

_____

_____

_____

_____

Be sure to take your Ultimate Babysitting Kit and manual to each babysitting job! The parents who hire you trust you to take excellent care of their children while they are away.

THE PARENTS' RESPONSIBILITIES

Like we said, the babysitter's responsibility is not to replace the parent—you won't be giving direction to how the children grow. Rather, you are implementing the parenting technique of the children's primary caregiver. They should also have a certain level of responsibility towards you. So, before you start any job, make sure that the parent retains their primary responsibilities, which include:

1. **Arrangements**—the parents should arrange for your

arrival time and transportation and tell you what time they will be home. The parents should call you if they are delayed and arrange for a safe way for you to get home.

2. **Give you specific duties**—some parents will want you to do some basic chores while they are away— this could mean, along with watching the children, that they may also expect you to do dishes or tidy up toys. Remember that babysitting is your main job, but you should attempt to keep things tidy too.

3. **Give clear instructions**—the parents should fill out the Ultimate Babysitting Emergency Contact form with you before they leave, as doing so will help you reach them in case of an emergency.

You should also be given instructions on meal times, snacks, and what foods and drinks should be eaten and when.

Parents should tell their children, in front of you, that *you* are in charge, and that the children need to follow *your* rules. Also, the parents should give you specific information about the children's naptime and bedtime routine, including:

- Time to go to bed
- Pajamas
- Lights or night light
- Bedtime stories or prayers
- A bedtime snack

The parents should let you know if you can have snacks, use their computer or TV, etc.

The parents will likely expect you to:

- Supervise their children at all times
- Follow routines and rules
- Watch for hazards
- Prepare simple snacks and meals
- Tidy up
- Play with the children
- Call them if there are any issues

YOUR RESPONSIBILITIES

As a babysitter, you are in charge of the children while the parents are away.

- You are responsible for the safety and well-being of the children
- You are to be dependable
- You should not have friends over while babysitting
- You should never leave the children alone
- You should keep phone calls short
- You should follow the parents' routines
- You should know and practice safety rules.

YOUR EXPECTATIONS (what things do you expect to happen while babysitting?)

YOUR PARENTS' EXPECTATIONS

You should always check with your parents before accepting

a babysitting job.

Your parents should know:

- Whom you are babysitting for
- The times you are babysitting (from when to when)
- How you will get there and get home

If you ever suspect the parent of the child you are babysitting has been drinking alcohol, do not get a ride home with them. Call your parents and ask them to pick you up. Discuss this ahead of time with your parents and have a code phrase for emergencies, such as "Could you pick me up because I need to shop at the grocery store on the way home."

Your parents should know that phrase means that the parents you are babysitting for have been drinking and your parents should come and get you right away.

CHILDREN'S EXPECTATIONS

By now, you should have formed a bond with the children you babysit. As a result, they will be more excited when they hear you are coming. They will expect you to be a fun and happy babysitter. This will be the case if you have proven yourself to be a kind, reliable, and caring individual.

As a babysitter, your role in their life should not be to bring any form of disruption because children are in their formative years. Conflicting messages in the approach to their upbringing communicates discord and disorder. If you have teenagers in the house, your acts of defiance against what the parents say may encourage defiance in them as well. It is crucial to understand that the children look up to you with the same respect to authority as they do to their parents/caregivers.

They will feel safe and comfortable with you IF:

- You know the household routines and rules
- You spend all your time with them
- You are genuinely interested in them
- You read to them, play with them, and keep them safe

The children will tell their parents if you were a good babysitter. If the kids like you and tell their parents so, their parents will most likely call you again to babysit.

PROFESSIONALISM AND RESPECTING DIFFERENCES

Professionalism means a person who is qualified in a profession. You are qualified because you have taken the Ultimate Babysitting Course! Babysitting is a huge responsibility.

Since you are taking the Ultimate Babysitting Course, you are one step ahead of becoming professional. You have educated yourself, have an Emergency Contact form, and you've been trained on how to watch out for hazards and what to do in an emergency.

The parents are also looking for you to be professional, mature, kind, caring, honest, and dependable.

Here are some tips you can follow for behaving in a professional manner:

- Arrive early and prepared
- Dress appropriately; make sure you are clean and presentable
- Have the parents fill out the emergency contact info sheet
- Take a tour of the house to look for safety hazards
- Do more than is expected of you (i.e. tidying up, dishes, toys)
- Follow through on promises (i.e. taking the kids to the park)
- Keep a smile on your face and the right attitude in your heart
- When the parents get home, thank them for the babysitting job

RESPECTING DIVERSITY

In North America, families come from many different backgrounds and reflect a wide range of cultures, languages, lifestyles, and religions.

Some of the families that you will be babysitting for may be from another country, dress differently than you, or eat different foods. They may attend a different church, pray before meals or bedtime, or celebrate holidays differently.

Remember your job is to look after the children. Be respectful of differences, and remember to stay open-minded. Even better would be to take the time to learn new things!

SIBLINGS

Your goal when babysitting is to keep the children safe and have a fun time together. The best way to keep the children happy is to set the stage for success by planning beforehand the things you will do together. If you keep the kids occupied, there should be less time for boredom and trouble.

The best way to keep the energy happy and positive is by positive reinforcement. This means to praise the children for their good behaviour, good ideas, and how well they play and get along. Treat the children equally. Siblings spend a great deal of time together and know each other very well. One minute they can be laughing and colouring, and in an instant, they can be fighting over the mermaid blue crayon.

Ask the parents how they would like you to discipline the children and follow their rules. Have the parents say to the children before they leave that you are in charge. Some parents give timeouts, whereas some might suggest encouraging the kids to share and get along. **Never ever hit or threaten a child.**

If they continue to fight and argue, and you can't get them to behave, that will be when you should call their parents.

ARRIVE EARLY AND ARRIVE PREPARED

First impressions are important when babysitting. By arriving early and being prepared, you will set the stage for success when the parents are away. You will have time to ask questions and get organized. If everyone is rushed, you could potentially forget to fill out the emergency form.

BABYSITTER CHECKLIST

✓ THE ULTIMATE BABYSITTING KIT

✓ THE ULTIMATE BABYSITTING MANUAL

✓ Have the parents fill out the Emergency Contact Information Sheet

✓ Map out an emergency escape route

✓ Food and drink list

✓ Special request(s)

✓ Telephone Interview Sheet with details

IMPORTANCE OF FOLLOWING A ROUTINE

Schedules and routines are important for children because they like predictability and need to know what's coming next. If their schedule is consistent and predictable, they will behave better and also feel safe. Once a pattern is established, (for instance, that lunch comes after playtime) they will easily cooperate.

Schedules help build trust between parents and children, which still applies to babysitters and children. The children know that the adult in charge will take care of them. When children are thrust around with no schedule and unknowns, they will start to feel anxiety and worry. Once they feel that way, they can also become irritable and misbehave. Some flexibility is important, but try to stick to the parents' routine as closely as possible!

THE ULTIMATE BABYSITTING COURSE KIT

Your kit should include:

- A nice babysitting bag
- An emergency contact information pad
- Emergency numbers
- First aid kit
- Notepad
- Pen
- Nut-free granola bar
- Bottled water
- Tissues

You should add these items to your ultimate babysitter kit:

- Cellphone, if you have one
- $10.00 for an emergency taxi
- A game, such as UNO™
- A book, such as Dr. Seuss "The Cat in the Hat"
- A colouring book and crayons
- A small toy, puzzle, or some Lego®
- An appropriate movie, such as a Disney one

You should always bring your Ultimate Babysitting Course manual and journal to every babysitting job for quick reference.

> "You'll miss the **BEST** things if you keep your **EYES SHUT!**"
> - Dr Seuss

BEAUTIFUL BABIES
(BIRTH - 12 MONTHS)

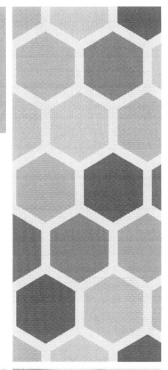

CHAPTER ONE: BEAUTIFUL BABIES, BIRTH TO ONE YEAR

*B*abies are special. Even though they can't talk yet, they will communicate to you in other ways. When you are babysitting a baby, make sure you talk, smile, and sing often. Your job as a babysitter is to provide the best possible care by meeting all their needs. Never take your eyes off babies! Although, since they are just so darn cute, you probably won't want to.

Pros of babysitting infants:

- You get a chance to watch a child develop

- They are sleeping more often than not

- Gives the primary caregivers a break

- You can do some other work while you watch the baby

Cons of babysitting infants:

- Colicky infants can be challenging

- Most parents are not comfortable leaving newborns with other people

PARENTAL EXPECTATIONS FOR INFANTS

A baby (birth to one year) may do any of the following:

- reach for objects
- hold small toys
- lift chest off the ground
- roll over
- put hands, fingers, and objects in their mouth
- roll, wiggle, and creep toward toys
- hold their head steady once they are about six months old
- grab at objects
- creep, crawl, and sit up
- crawl upstairs, but not down
- play shy
- pull up to a steady position around 9 - 12 months old
- try to walk around furniture while holding on to it
- babble and "coo"
- be expressive while trying to communicate with you

Infants are born with natural reflexes, such as:

- Sucking—babies know instantly how to suckle a nipple and receive nourishment
- The root reflex—when you stroke a baby's cheek, they will turn in that direction to suckle
- The startle reflex—if the baby hears a loud noise, they throw back their head, arms, and legs, then pull themselves back up.
- Grasp reflex—the baby will grasp onto your finger

RECOMMENDATIONS FOR BABYSITTERS

Remember that it's normal for babies to cry, which is how they communicate. Therefore, you should make sure to keep them:

- Dry
- Warm
- Comfortable
- Fed
- Gas-free by burping
- Nap on schedule

Infants are special, and only the most experienced babysitters should babysit babies and infants. If you accept a job that requires babysitting a baby from birth to 12 months, be prepared to give them extra time, love, care, and attention. Caring for an infant is a major responsibility.

Here are a few more facts about babies.

- Digestive systems are delicate and food routines need to be kept
- Vision and hearing are limited
- Muscles are developing, meaning they are weak and uncoordinated at this stage
- Bones are soft
- There is a soft spot on their head called the "fontanel"
- Body temperatures change quickly; they can get hot or cold very fast. Therefore, it's important to dress them properly.

Vocabulary to use: Before babies learn to talk, they babble and "coo." Children begin to produce sentences or partial sentences and phrases when they have learned about 50 words.

Music: Babies love music. Play quiet music and sing to the baby. Sing songs while you go about your routines. Babies need reassurance that they are safe and loved. Talk and sing in a gentle voice, and smile sweetly when taking care of them.

Playing with sounds: baby talk is similar all over the world!

Fingerplays: You can play Peek-a-boo with a baby. Hide your face behind your hands. Then, move them out of the way and say, "peek-a-boo" to the baby. This game establishes a trust that you are always going to come back.

Baby talk at three months:

- The baby listens to your voice as you talk.
- Turns towards other voices, sounds, and music.
- By the end of three months, babies begin coo-ing (which is a happy little sound).

Baby talk at six months:

- The baby begins babbling with different sounds. For example: "baba" or "dada."
- By the end of six months, babies should recognize their own name.

Baby talk at nine months:

- After nine months, babies understand a few basic words, like "no" and "bye bye."

Baby talk at twelve months:

- Most babies say a few simple words, like "mama and dada."
- Babies understand short, one-step requests, such as "Put that down."

Holding: When babysitting an infant, you will be doing a lot of lifting, holding, and cuddling the baby. It is essential to learn how to pick up and hold a baby properly. Most babies like being held, though a few may not. It may take a little time to warm up to you. Be gentle and respectful when holding a baby, and it's important to be calm and confident before you pick them up. Take your time, smile, and relax because this is supposed to be fun! Don't worry too much; you will get used to it.

Cradle Hold

The cradle hold is one of the most popular and natural ways to hold a baby.

- Talk or sing in a quiet and gentle voice.
- Tell the baby, "I'm going to pick you up now."
- Place one hand under the baby's bottom.

- Use your other hand to support the baby's neck and head.
- Lift the baby slowly and gently, and hold them near your body.
- Your arms should create a cozy hammock or cradle for the baby to rest in.

Using the cradle hold lets you look and talk to the newborn.

To place the baby down in the crib or car seat:

- gently place the baby down and slide out your hands.
- be gentle, smile, and sing to the baby.

Shoulder Hold

A baby loves to nestle up against your shoulder and will have a nice lookout when they are awake and a comfy spot when they are asleep. This is also the hold you will use when burping a baby.

I find the shoulder hold to be another very natural way to hold a baby. Remember that a small baby cannot support nor hold their head up until after six months of age! Be very careful when handling a newborn baby's head, especially around the fontanel, which is the soft spot on the top of his/her head.

- Slide one hand gently under the baby's head for support.
- Slide your other hand under the bottom.
- Once you have a good hold, slowly and gently scoop the baby up and bring them to your chest.
- Rest the baby on your chest and shoulder, supporting the head and neck.
- Keep your other hand under the baby's bottom.
- The baby should love this. In this hold, they should be able to hear your heartbeat and see over your shoulder.

To keep the baby safe, never hold hot drinks or cook while you are holding a baby. Always go slowly and hold the baby securely when going up or down stairs!

Diapers

Babies can go through as many as ten diapers per day, and it's important to change a baby's diaper often to avoid diaper rash. Change their diaper immediately after a pee or bowel movement, and never let the baby sit in a soiled dirty diaper.

It's a good idea to ask the baby's parents to demonstrate how they like their baby's diaper changed because each parent may have a slightly different style. Changing diapers is not difficult and gets easier every time. Practice on a doll so you can get more comfortable.

The secret to changing a diaper to be prepared!

You will need:

- Change table, or change pad

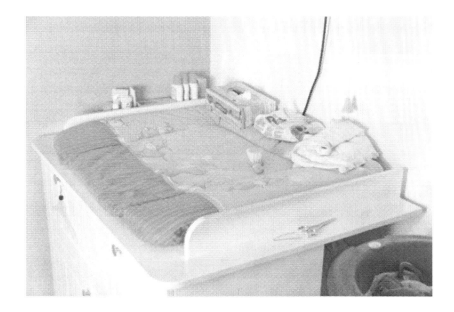

- Two clean diapers

- Baby wipes, or a warm damp cloth

- Cream, Vaseline, baby powder, and/or diaper rash cream (depending on what the parents use)

- A burp cloth

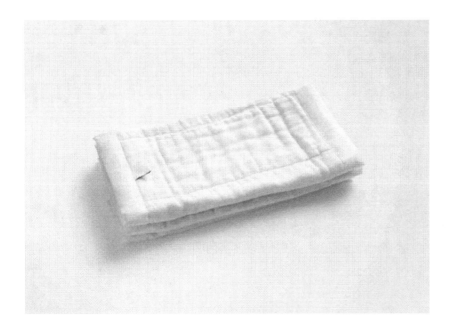

- A receiving blanket

- A towel for drying

- A garbage bin close by

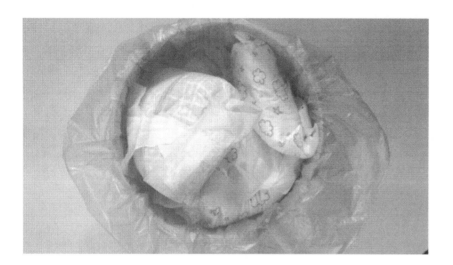

Remember that you should never leave the baby alone on a change table or bed when changing a diaper; the baby could squirm or roll off when you are not looking. If the phone rings or the doorbell goes off, don't answer it until the baby is in a safe place. The caller will leave a message or wait.

The baby is your top priority. Be sure to secure the safety straps, seatbelt, and guard rails on the change table, and always, *always* leave one hand on the baby to keep them safe.

Talk or sing softly to the baby and tell them …

We are going to change your bum now! Fa la la la la

STEPS TO CHANGE A DIAPER

There is no other way to say this: Anyone babysitting an infant in diapers must be able and willing to change diapers. This is crucial to the child's wellbeing and is in line with the duties you can expect in your job. Some parents will ask if you are willing to perform this duty, whereas others will assume that you are because it is part of caring for the infant. However, if you are *not* comfortable with this task, you must bring up your concerns and let the parents make an informed choice.

How to change a diaper:

HOW TO CHANGE DIAPER

1. Wash your hands!
2. Lay the baby down on the change table, on their back. Do up the straps, seat belt, or guardrail (depending on the change table's set up.
3. Take off the wet or dirty diaper by unfastening the diaper tabs and set the diaper out of the way. There will usually be a garbage or diaper genie close by. Don't let the baby touch or play with the soiled

diaper, and don't leave the baby alone just to throw the diaper out.

4. With one hand, gently grab the baby's ankles to lift the legs and hips. Clean the baby's bottom with a diaper wipe or warm cloth.

5. Wipe a baby girl's bum from front to back to prevent infection.

6. When changing a boy's baby diaper, keep a receiving blanket close in case he decides to pee. If he does pee, it will spray all over, and you might have to start over and you may even have to change his clothing! If he pees while you're changing him, put the receiving blanket over the pee.

7. Slide a fresh new diaper under the baby's bottom. The sticky tabs should be on either side of the baby's hips. Apply any lotion, Vaseline or diaper cream, or powder now.

8. Remove the tabs to expose the sticky part. Most diapers today have colourful pictures that will let you see the front and back easily.

9. Hold the diaper in the front of their tummy and pull the tabs around their belly to fasten.

10. Be careful not to fasten too tight, or the baby might get a tummy ache. Likewise, be careful not to fasten too loosely or pee/poo might squirt out later.

11. Pick up the baby and place them in a safe place, such as their crib, playpen, or baby seat.

12. Wash your hands with warm, soapy water. Since

babies love to use their hands to feel around, then put them in their mouth, you should also wash the baby's hands with a warm washcloth.

Congratulations! You have successfully changed a baby's diaper. Don't worry if it's a bit difficult at first; it will get easier every time!

DRESSING THE BABY IN PJS OR CLOTHING

Babies can be messy; they drool and slobber a lot, and often need their clothing changed several times per day. Dressing a baby is a piece of cake—that is, after you've learned a few tricks for getting their head, arms, and legs through the tiny neck, arm, and leg holes.

If you need to change the baby's clothes, and the parents haven't left any clothing out, choose something simple, comfortable, and easy to put on, such as a sleeper. This is not the time for any of their special occasion outfits. Most babies wear onesies under their sleepers, which—in baby terms—are undershirts that button up under their bum to keep them snug.

Before you start:

- Get all the clothing out together.
- A onesie and a sleeper are generally appropriate during any season.

- Most babies don't like being naked because they feel cold, unprotected, and uncomfortable.

Steps for changing a baby's clothes:

1. Lay the baby down on their back.
2. Remove old clothing by carefully pulling their arms and legs through the openings.
3. Be gentle with their head and support it with one hand.
4. Lay the new sleeper down and place the baby on top.
5. Place your hand under their back and head, then gently put the head through the onesie.
6. Pull it over the baby's body as they lay there.
7. Lift a leg, one at a time, and insert each into the sleeper.
8. A sleeper with feet already in is a better choice than one without feet and requiring separate socks.
9. The baby's arms and legs are very flexible, but be gentle and confident while changing the baby
10. Sing and smile at the baby as you change their clothes. Singing softly will reassure the baby that all is well. Don't worry or be rattled if they fuss or cry.
11. I like to wrap babies in a fuzzy blanket after they are changed.
12. Cradle the baby and say, "All done! Good job."
13. Put the dirty clothing in the laundry room.

Congratulations! You have now successfully changed the baby's clothes! As it is with diapers, it gets easier with practice.

FEEDING THE BABY (AND BABY BOTTLES)

Babies eat every few hours. Most babies will be on a set feeding schedule, and new foods would have been introduced to the baby during the first year.

Here are some guidelines for what you can feed a typical baby when you are babysitting.

Always wash your hands before handling the baby's bottle or food.

Birth to four months:

- The baby receives breast milk or formula only, every few hours.
- The baby will use their "rooting reflex" and turn their head and open their mouth, looking for a nipple.
- The baby's digestive tract is developing, and they have no teeth. That is why they receive liquids only.
- The mother/parents will have a schedule in terms of how much and how often. For example, a three-month-old baby may require 4oz. of formula every three hours.

- If the baby is drinking formula, the parents will most likely have the bottles pre-mixed and ready. If not, mix the formula according to the parents' instructions.
- Formula will come in powder, liquid, or breast milk.
- Follow the parents' instructions for warming the bottle. Hot spots can occur when heating the bottle. Always test the temperature of the bottle by dabbing some on your wrist; you never want to burn the baby's mouth. The milk should be lukewarm.
- Microwave bottle heating is not recommended, though you should still follow the parents' rules on heating.
- Gently shake the bottle to ensure it's mixed and heated evenly throughout.
- Sit down with the baby in your arms. Their head should be in the nook of your arm.
- Tilt the bottle so the nipple is full of milk.
- Don't force the nipple in their mouth. Let the baby smell the milk. Gently rub their cheek, and the baby will root in that direction and want to suckle the bottle.
- If the baby is fussy or crying, take your time, console the baby, and start over.
- Don't rush the baby to eat. You and I don't like being rushed, and neither do babies.
- If the baby rejects the nipple and spits it out, such could tell you a few things. In some cases, the

nipple might be clogged or the formula could be too hot. If either of these cases occurs, start over. Try to work with the parents' schedule as much as possible, but don't force the baby to finish the bottle; their little belly might be full. Let the liquid sit in the baby for a few minutes and settle (i.e. don't start playing right away or the baby might spit it all up).

- Throw out any leftover milk and put the bottle in the sink or dishwasher.

BURPING A BABY

Ask the parents how they like to burp their baby. Some babies burp partway through the bottle, whereas some may at the end. Follow the parents' burping instructions.

- Burping a baby is easy, just take your time. You can sit a baby up and place a cloth under their chin (support their head and hold their face in your hands) and, ever so gently, pat or rub their back. Another burping technique is a shoulder hold—if you burp the baby using the shoulder hold, put a receiving blanket over your shoulder first.
- There may be some spitting up. As with the previous tip, remember to take your time and not rush
- Never leave a baby alone with a bottle or prop a

bottle up. The baby could throw up and choke on their own vomit.

Feeding babies aged four to six months

When babies are between four and six months old, they will start to show signs of being ready to try solid baby food. Each baby is unique, and the parents will direct you on feeding baby food.

Some signs a baby four- to six-month-old is ready to try baby food:

- Can hold their head up
- Sit well in a high chair
- Make chewing motions
- Show weight gain
- Gained an interest in food
- Close their mouth around a spoon
- Still seems hungry after eight to ten feedings of breast milk or liquids
- Teething

After four months, babies will still drink breast milk or formula, along with a pureed baby food, such as squash, sweet potatoes, apples, bananas, peaches, pears, and iron-fortified pabulum cereal.

Feeding a Baby:

1. Open the baby food, making sure you hear the jar "pop."
2. Place the food in a small container.
3. Heat and warm the foods per the parents' instructions (baby foods can be served cold, at room temperature, or heated).
4. Some families place the container in hot water and wait; other families will use the microwave oven. Be careful if using the microwave to heat the food because it can heat up unevenly and create hot spots.
5. Stir and taste the food yourself before feeding it to the baby.
6. Gather everything you will need on a table beside the high chair (bib, baby food, spoon, warm washcloth).
7. Place the baby in the high chair and fasten the straps/seat belt.
8. Put a tiny amount on the baby spoon and hold it close to the baby's mouth. The baby should open up. Take your time with this step.
9. Don't expect the baby to eat all the food—when a baby cries or turns away from food, that means they are full.
10. Pay attention to their body language because they can't speak yet.
11. Wipe the baby up and let them sit for five minutes to settle; do not leave the room or leave the baby alone in the high chair.
12. Throw out unused food.

13. Put the dishes and utensils in the sink.
14. Wash your hands.
15. Wash the baby with a warm washcloth.

How Much Do Babies Eat? (4 - 6 months)

Begin with 1 tablespoon of puree or cereal, then mix with 4-5 tablespoons of breast milk or formula; it will be very runny. As children get older, their parents will likely start to increase the amount of solid food and lessen the amount of liquid food. The parents will tell you how to do it.

FEEDING BABIES AGED SIX TO EIGHT MONTHS:

Signs of readiness are the same as four to six months. Babies this age will eat:

- Breast milk or formula
- Pureed or strained fruits (bananas, pears, applesauce, peaches)
- Pureed or strained veggies (avocado, well-cooked carrots, squash, and sweet potato)

How Much Do Babies Eat? (aged 6 to 8 months)

At this stage, they will probably be eating very small amounts; about 1 tablespoon of fruit, 1 tablespoon vegetables, and 3-9 tablespoons of pabulum.

Feeding Babies aged eight to ten months:

Signs of readiness

- Same as six to eight months
- Pick up objects with thumb and forefinger
- Can transfer items from one hand to the other
- Put everything in their mouth
- Move their jaw in a chewing motion

What to feed?

Breast milk or formula, along with:

- A small amount of soft cheese or cottage cheese
- Mashed fruit and vegetables
- Finger foods
- Small pieces of banana, scrambled eggs, well-cooked
- Yellow squash, peas, potato, corn, low sugar O-shaped cereal, lightly toasted toast, or bagels, cut up
- Small amounts of protein (eggs, pureed meats, chicken)
- Fish, tofu, well-cooked mashed beans, lentils, peas
- Iron-fortified cereal

How Much Do Babies Eat? (8 - 10 months)

They will usually eat about ¼-⅓ cup of the cheese, cereal, fruit, vegetables, and ⅛ cup protein.

FEEDING BABIES AGED TEN TO TWELVE MONTHS:

- Shows signs of readiness (same as eight to ten months) plus:
- Swallows food more easily
- More teeth
- No longer pushes food out to ooze down face
- Tries to use a spoon

What to feed

Breast milk or formula, along with:

- Soft cheese, yogurt, cottage cheese
- No milk until one-year-old
- Fruit and/or cheese cut into small cubes
- Bite-sized soft cooked veggies (pears, carrots, corn)
- Combo food (Macaroni and cheese)
- Finger food; lighted toasted bread or bagels, small pieces of ripe
- Banana, scrambled eggs, spiral pasta, teething crackers or biscuits, low sugar O-shaped cereal
- Iron-fortified cereals

HOW MUCH DO BABIES EAT? (10-12 MONTHS)

⅛ cup to ½ cup (small servings)

Each baby is unique, and the parents will probably give you a feeding schedule. Be sure to write it down and follow as closely as you can!

Feeding time is also fun and social, so remember to take your time and don't rush. Wipe up the baby with a warm soapy washcloth, wash your hands, and tidy up once you're done!

Great job! Well done! Bravo!

SLEEPING

Here's a guideline about how much babies sleep!

Every baby is special with different sleeping habits. The following is a guideline for how much babies sleep. Sleep is important because it's what allows them to grow and develop.

SLEEP CHART GUIDELINES

	Night	Naps	Total Sleep
Newborn to 2 Months	8-9 Hours	4-5 Hours (3 Naps)	14-16 Hours
2 to 4 Months	9-10 Hours	4-5 Hours (3 Naps)	14-16 Hours
4 to 6 Months	10 Hours	4-5 Hours (2-3 Naps)	14-15 Hours
6 to 9 Months	10-11 Hours	3-4 Hours (2 Naps)	14 Hours
9 to 12 Months	10-12 Hours	2-3 Hours (2 Naps)	14 Hours
12 to 18 Months	11-12 Hours	2-3 Hours (1-2 Naps)	13-14 Hours
18 Months to 2 Years	11 Hours	2 Hours (1 Nap)	13-14 Hours
2 to 3 Years	10-11 Hours	1-2 Hours (1 Nap)	12-14 Hours
3 to 5 Years	10-11 Hours	1 Nap	11-13 Hours
5 to 12 Years		Usually, stops napping by age 5	10-11 Hours

BABY SLEEPING TIPS

Newborn - 2 months: SLEEP TIPS

- Newborns sleep 2 to 4 hours and wake up hungry.
- Babies tend to look restless and stir while sleeping; they smile, move their arms and legs, and look like they might wake up at any second.
- Newborns don't know how to soothe themselves to sleep; you can't spoil a newborn. It's okay to help them by giving them a pacifier, swaddling, rocking, gently rubbing their back, or cuddling with them until they doze off.
- Try to be quiet, keep the lights dim, and don't engage with them by talking or making eye contact.

2 - 4 MONTHS: SLEEP TIPS

- Babies at this age may sleep for a six-hour stretch at night.
- Parents probably have pre-bedtime/naptime routines like bathing, feeding, song time, soft music, etc.

Each parent should advise you on the best way to tuck the baby in.

4 - 6 MONTHS: SLEEP TIPS

- Babies at this age can sleep through the night without nighttime feeding. Sometimes, they may sleep between six to twelve hours at a time.
- Research shows that 60% of babies sleep straight through the night by six months. 80% sleep through the night by nine months.

6 - 12 MONTHS: SLEEP TIPS

- Some babies wake up and want "mommy."
- It's okay to soothe a crying baby by rubbing their back or cuddling them in a rocking chair.

When putting a baby down for a nap, the parents will most likely give you steps and a routine to follow, such as:

- Eating lunch
- Bottle
- Naptime with soother at 12:30 to approximately 2:30

Other important information when putting the baby down for a nap:

- When babies are sleepy, they may rub their eyes or suck their thumbs.

- Use a soft and gentle voice when tucking a baby in for a nap.
- Make sure the crib has nothing in it.
- Place the baby in their crib, always on their back.
- Make sure the sides of the crib are locked.
- Use the baby or video monitor.
- If you are doing homework or listening to music, keep it soft so you can hear the baby if they wake up.
- Quietly check the baby often, about every ten minutes.

The parents will tell you the best way to put their baby down for a nap. Write down their instructions and follow them carefully.

WHEN BABIES CRY

Babies cry to communicate their feelings through gestures and sounds, so never disregard a crying child. Even if it is a tantrum, you must take care to ascertain there is nothing physically wrong with the baby and not assume they are fine just because you are irritated by the crying.

Babies cannot talk, and the only way they can communicate to you is by crying. So, you should try to look at crying as a good thing! It means the baby is trying to tell you something.

Things to check if the baby is crying:

- Are they hungry?
- Is their diaper dirty or wet?
- Are they tired and ready for a nap?
- Do they want to be held and cuddled?
- Do they have a tummy ache and need to burp?
- Too cold or too hot?
- Teething?
- Over-stimulated, too much noise, and toys?
- Do they want more stimulation?
- Not feeling well?

If you've tried everything (feeding, changing the diapers, walking, rocking, cuddling, given toys, burped) and the baby is still fussy and crying, don't fret and stay calm. If you get wound up and tense, the baby will sense it and cry more.

If the crying persists, place the baby on their back in their crib and let them fuss for a minute. Take a few deep breaths and remind yourself that you can handle this. **Never ever shake a baby**. Shaking a baby can damage their brain or even cause death. Just take a break, tune it out, and start over. Their crying will pass.

If all else fails and the baby cries for more than 30 minutes, call the parents and ask what to do. As a mom, I would want to know. The parents will talk you through it or come home. You can also call your own mom for tips on handling the situation.

Quiet Time

When things get hectic and it's not close to bedtime or naptime, it's okay to bring the intensity down a few notches and have some "quiet time."

After a few active hours of playing and following a routine, you might want to try to implement some quiet time. Quiet time occurs well before naptime or bedtime. It is a time to recharge, read a book, and relax.

1. Dim the lights.
2. Turn off the TV.
3. Pick up a Dr. Seuss book, cozy up, and read it to the baby, slowly.
4. Aim for 30 minutes of quiet time.
5. Let the child look at the book and the pictures.
6. Give the child something to look forward to at the end, such as a snack (i.e. "in half-an-hour, when quiet time is over, we can have a snack!").

Everyone can benefit from some downtime. You will find that, after a bit of quiet time, the child will become much sweeter.

Play Time

Small babies love interacting with people. They like anything that appeals to their senses of sight, sound, and touch.

Babies love:

- Faces and voices
- Singing gently
- Smiling

Place the baby on the floor, on their back, and on a blanket. When in this position, they will wiggle and talk and get some baby exercise.

The baby may enjoy:

- Brightly coloured soft toys
- Musical toys
- Rattles
- Squeaky toys
- Big blocks

Games to play with the baby:

- Patty cake
- Peek-a-boo
- This little piggy …

Babies like to touch:

- Soft blankets; they particularly like hugging them
- Your shirt
- Anything soft
- Cloth books or blocks

SET THE STAGE FOR SUCCESS

It is in your best interests to ensure that the environment in the home is conducive for your success. Parents may overlook some things (though, not on purpose), but you can catch the missing aspects in time because you are a specialized child caregiver. Make your first baby sitting session a mission to figure out what you need to do to keep the kids engaged, comfortable, and having a good time, even as their parents are away. Subsequent sessions will be more relaxed, owing to what you found out that first day.

Keeping Babies Safe

You must always keep your focus on the baby. The only safe place for a baby to be, while you use the bathroom or check on the other children, is in their crib and on their back. Babies love to touch and hold things, then put the object in their mouth; therefore, all playthings should be too large to swallow.

Things to keep in mind when caring for babies:

- Toys have no sharp edges or points.
- Keep all plastic bags, cords, and pillows away from infants and small children.
- Buttons, pins, barrettes, and bobby pins are all dangerous for babies and small children.

- Avoid items like long strings or cords that could strangle the baby.
- Look for small objects on the floor that the baby could swallow.

Babies are also in danger for the following:

- **Falling**—never leave a baby alone on a change table, couch, chair, or high chair.
- **Safe Place**—if you must leave to check something in another room, take the baby with you or place them in their crib on their back where it is safe.
- **Safety Strap**—always use a safety strap or belt when sitting the baby in a high chair, change table, or stroller.
- **Crib**—check the crib before putting the baby in it; never put a pillow or blanket in the crib because babies can smother under the weight.
- **Burns**—never hold an infant when eating or drinking; the food or drink could fall on the baby and burn them. Place the baby down in a safe place first.
- **Fingers**—watch that the baby's fingers don't get caught in doors, cupboards, drawers, the refrigerator, or the stove. Babies love to explore everything, but you should never take your eyes off them for a second.
- **Electrical outlets**—never let a baby play near or

stick any toys into an electrical outlet. The parents should have installed safety caps on electrical outlets.

- **Drowning**—you should never agree to take a baby swimming or give a baby a bath, and tell the parents you are uncomfortable doing so. Babies can be scalded and burned by hot water or, even worse, drown. Babies can drown within just an inch of water. A clean face cloth in lukewarm water is what you should use to wash a baby's face and hands. If there is a large bowel movement and a big messy poop to clean up, a few washcloths will do.

"A person's a person no matter how SMALL!

- dr. seuss

TODDLERS
(1-3 YEARS)

CHAPTER TWO: TODDLERS (1 - 3 YEARS)

*T*oddlers are aged one to three years or twelve to thirty-six months. Toddlers are very active and love to explore, walk, and move around.

At the toddler stage, the child's vocabulary is expanding. They will most likely understand you, though they still only have a few words to say themselves.

Pros of babysitting a toddler:

- They are more active
- They communicate more
- Love to have creative fun
- There is a wider array of activities to do with them

Cons of babysitting a toddler:

- They can be challenging when it comes to obedience

PARENTAL EXPECTATIONS FOR TODDLERS

A toddler (aged 1 - 3) may do/be any of the following:

- Walk
- Crawl
- Creep
- Roll
- Run
- Feed themselves
- Determined to try everything on their own
- Climb on furniture and up the stairs
- Dance to music
- Try to dress or undress themselves

- Try to wash their face or brush their teeth
- Pretend to talk on the phone
- Scold the family pet
- Use a banana as a telephone
- Enjoy action TV characters, like *Bob the Builder*

TODDLER VOCABULARY

Between ages one to three, a toddler's vocabulary will go through extraordinary growth. In that time, the toddler will go from speaking a few simple words to:

- Putting words in phrases
- Saying sentences
- Asking questions
- Laughing lots!

Toddler's Words (12 - 18 months):

- Understands about 100 words
- May speak between three to twenty words
- Says "Mama" and "Dada"
- Points to objects and names them (i.e. dog, cat, baby, uh-oh, "all gone," more)
- Responds to questions by nodding their head for yes or shaking their head no
- Imitates words and facial expressions

- Babbles in jargon

Toddlers' Words (18 - 24 months):

- Understands approximately 300 words
- Can say about 50 words
- Names familiar objects, such as "cat" and "ball"
- Enjoys waving and saying "hi" and "bye"
- Listens when someone reads a book to them
- Can identify approximately five body parts when asked (i.e. eye, nose, arm, hair, head)
- Combines words to make two-word sentences

Toddlers' Words (18 - 36 months):

- Understands approximately 500 words
- Can say approximately 200 words
- Can put together three words into a sentence
- Understands "hot," "big," and "little"
- When asked questions with simple answers, they are likely to know or have a good guess when answering (i.e. "What does a cow do?" *it moos*; "What does a dog do?" *it will bark*)
- May enjoy saying "all gone"

By thirty-six months, toddlers can understand around 900 words and can usually say their own name.

It is important to read picture books and label things as you see them to the toddler. It is also important to talk in a normal and clear voice, pronouncing your words properly so the toddler understands. Baby talk drives toddlers nuts in the same way it would if someone used baby talk with an adult, so always speak to them as equals.

TODDLER TALK (AT **18** MONTHS):

- Most toddlers at this age can say at least 10 simple words
- Most toddlers can identify people or body parts when asked about them
- They like to repeat words or sounds as best they can
- They may mix up words and sounds, or shorten words (i.e. dog might sound like dawwww, noo'noo's, for noodles)

Toddler Talk (at 2-3 years):

By age two, toddlers have learned about 40 words. They may also start stringing them together in short phrases, like "me milk," "more milk," "mine ball," and "mine dawwg." By their third birthday, their vocabulary begins to expand rapidly.

It is important when communicating with the baby to smile, sing, talk clearly, read, and label things. The clearer you talk, the more likely a baby will learn to speak properly!

CARRYING A TODDLER

Toddlers are a busy bunch. They appear to have endless amounts of energy to explore and play all day long.

By eighteen months, toddlers can weigh between 9 to 14 kg (19.84 to 30.86 pounds). Once they turn three, they can weigh between 12 to 18 kg (26.46 to 39.68 pounds).

Toddlers don't always follow instructions at this point, so there may be times when carrying them is necessary.

I would encourage hand-holding and walking slowly, though sometimes you will need to carry them to your destination. If you are going out for a walk, it may be a good idea to use a stroller with a safety belt, since a toddler can bolt away in the blink of an eye. Some toddlers may still want to be carried everywhere and could follow you around lifting their arms, saying "up." The I-want-up syndrome is a signal that the child is feeling insecure and needs to be comforted to feel safe.

Since you are babysitting, this would make sense. I suggest carrying and sitting with the toddler until they feel safe enough to get down and explore. Cozy up on the couch, read a book, and watch their favourite TV show with them.

Be gentle and encouraging. Every time you go over to babysit and once the toddler has become more familiar with you, the need to be carried will wane away.

DIAPERS

Most toddlers still wear diapers. They may be too tall to change their diaper on a change table, but the parents will have a designated place where they change them. Check a toddler's diaper before and after naptime and after feedings. A toddler will be able to tell you when they have a dirty diaper. They will usually be co-operative and not like to be left in a messy dirty diaper.

Around twenty-four months (two years old) they could start showing signs of being ready for toilet training, but the fact is most toddlers wear diapers until age three.

Steps to change a toddler's diaper:

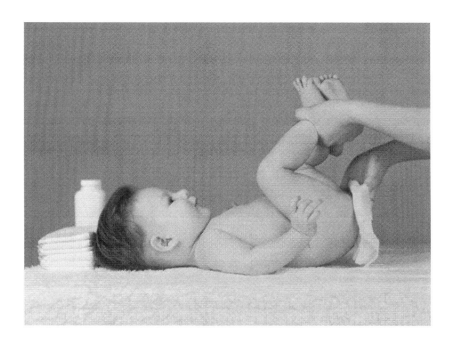

1. First, wash your hands!
2. Lay the toddler down on the change table, on their back. Do up the straps, seat belt, or guardrail.
3. Take off the wet or dirty diaper by unfastening the diaper tabs, then set the diaper out of the way. There will usually be a garbage bin or diaper genie close by. Do not let the toddler touch or play with the soiled diaper, and don't leave the toddler alone in the room when throwing the diaper out.
4. With one hand, gently grab the toddler's ankles to lift their legs and hips. Clean the child's bottom with a diaper wipe or warm cloth, and make sure you wipe a toddler girl's bum from front to back to prevent infection. When changing a little boy's diaper, keep a receiving blanket close in case he decides to pee. If he does pee, it will spray all over and you may have to start over changing his diaper and/or his clothing! If he pees while you are changing him, put the receiving blanket over the pee.
5. Slide a fresh and clean new diaper under the toddler's bottom. The sticky tabs should be on either side of the baby's hips. This would be the stage when you apply any lotion, Vaseline, or diaper cream or powder as required.
6. Remove the tabs to expose the sticky part. Most diapers today have colourful pictures that will let you see the front and back easily.
7. Hold the diaper on the front of their tummy and pull

the tabs around their belly to fasten. Be careful not to fasten too tight, or your toddler might have a tummy ache. Also be careful not to fasten too loosely or the pee/poo might squirt out.

8. Pick up the toddler and place them in a safe place like the crib, playpen, or baby seat.
9. Wash your hands with warm, soapy water. Since toddlers also love to use their hands to feel around, then put their hands in their mouth, you should wash the child's hands with a warm washcloth.

Congratulations! You have successfully changed the diaper. As it is with everything so far, it will get easier the more you do it.

DRESSING A TODDLER

Toddlers can go through many outfits in one day. The tot you are babysitting is walking, running, climbing, maybe trying to use the potty, touching everything from toothpaste to dog food, and eating. Toddlers insist on doing everything themselves and have a "I can do it!" mentality.

When selecting a clean outfit for the toddler to change into, look for something simple like track pants with no buttons or zippers. That way, they can pull it on themselves. If the toddler insists on dressing themselves, be encouraging and say things like "Great job!" "Excellent!" and "You can do it!" Remember to have patience.

If the toddler needs help to put on a new outfit or pajamas, take your time in following these steps. You do it yourself, so you can do it with the toddler.

To undress:

1. Undo the snaps, buttons, or zippers on the front of a shirt.
2. If the toddler is wearing a t-shirt or pullover, gently slide one arm out of each sleeve, then ease the shirt over the toddler's head. Be gentle around the ears and face.

To dress:

1. Put the shirt on in the same way. Undo the buttons or snaps.
2. Gently put one of the toddler's arms and hands through the first sleeve, then pull the shirt around their back and do the other one.
3. Do up the buttons or snaps.
4. To put a t-shirt on, give the neck a little stretch to allow the toddler's head to slip through easily. Be careful around the nose, ears, and face.
5. After their head pops through, gently guide each arm through the sleeves.

It may be a good idea to take some time and practice on a doll of some kind first. Don't forget to put the dirty clothing in the laundry room or hamper.

FEEDING TODDLERS

Age 1 - 3, or 12 - 36 months:

Note that, although the following are good guidelines, it is always necessary to discuss feeding habits and the child's diet with the parents. Make sure you follow their rules in terms of feeding.

- Toddlers eat every few hours. They won't be eating baby food anymore, and they like to sit in a high chair and feed themselves, usually using their fingers. You will need to cut their food up into small bite-size pieces. Remember that not all their teeth are in yet, meaning the toddler could easily choke.
- Feeding a meal or snack can take a while, as the toddler eats slowly and is learning to use their pincer grasp (thumb and forefinger). They feed themselves by picking up the food and bringing it to their mouth.
- Don't forget to put a bib on them and be prepared to clean the chair and the floor around them.
- Toddlers may show interest in trying to use a spoon to scoop up food as well.
- Always check if the parents approve giving their

child peanut butter or eggs, in case of a potential allergic reaction.

WHAT TO FEED TODDLERS

12 - 24 months:

- Whole milk
- Dairy products (cheese cut up in cubes, yogurt)
- Most of the same food the rest of the family eats (cut up small)
- Cereals
- Grains, whole wheat bread, pasta, rice
- Fruits: melons, grapes, watermelon, apples, oranges, and bananas. Remember to cut the fruit into small cubes. Fruit is easy for the toddler to feed to themselves and it won't cause them to choke.
- Vegetables: carrots, broccoli, cauliflower, corn, peas; cooked until soft and cut up in cubes (many parents give teething babies frozen peas or corn to chew on, which seems to help with the teething)
- Protein: eggs, meat, chicken (cooked and cut up into small bite-sized pieces).

Remember to always check with the parents before you feed the child anything.

How much do toddlers eat?

The parents will most likely give you instructions for how much they want you to feed their toddler; as a general rule, you can start with a small amount and replenish as they eat it. If you put a big portion on their high chair, you will most likely have a big portion to clean up from the floor later.

As an extra note about eggs, peanut butter, and other peanut products, it's good to keep in mind that some experts have controversial guidelines as to when to introduce these food items to children, as they may cause allergies. If you are unsure and if the parents have not introduced them to their toddler, it is **not** your place to do so either.

Another thing to keep in mind is that the number one food item that toddlers choke on is hot dogs! If feeding hot dogs to toddlers, you should always cut it both lengthwise AND sideways. Grapes are another choking hazard that you should cut small.

SOME SAFETY TIPS FOR FEEDING TODDLERS:

- Make sure the high chair is not near the stove, dishwasher, microwave or other appliances.
- Keep the high chair away from any walls so the child doesn't push their chair over.
- Always use the safety strap in the chair.
- Don't let the child stand on their high chair.

- Always cut the food into small cubes to avoid choking.
- Always use the high chair for feeding time. A child can choke quite easily by running with food in their mouth.
- Ask the parents what drinks should be given to them before, during, and after mealtime. Toddlers seem to eat less if taken before, which is perfectly normal. By serving the drink after eating, they won't fill up on liquids.

A daycare where I worked at in college always had the toddlers have a big drink at the end of each meal. They had one incident where a child woke up from a nap, packed their cheeks like a chipmunk, and didn't swallow the food. It was very scary, as the food could have dislodged during their sleep and choked the child.

SLEEPING

Toddlers are very active and require between 12 - 14 hours of sleep over a 24-hour period.

SLEEPCHART GUIDELINES

Age	Night Time Sleep	Naps	Total
12-18 Months	10-12 Hours	2-3 Hours (2 Naps)	14 Hours
18-24 Months	11 Hours	1-2 Hours (1 Nap)	13-14 Hours
2-3 Years	10-11 Hours	1-2 Hours Nap	12-14 Hours

TODDLERS' SLEEPING TIPS:

Toddlers have many changes in a day. It is important to keep on parents' schedule as closely as possible. Between the ages of one to three years, a toddler will typically go from having two naps a day to one afternoon nap. Toddlers also may move from a crib to a bed.

Help the toddler prepare for naptime or bedtime by choosing quiet activities and following the parents' routine. You can tell when a toddler is getting sleepy, when they rub their eyes, stumble, become short-tempered, or become over-excited.

Let the toddler give you the right cues before you put them down. A child who is not sleepy will not go to bed easily, no matter how often you try to get them to sleep. In the end, it becomes frustrating for both you and the child, and you may end up in an unhappy and more difficult situation. You also won't want the child to associate you with forcing them to do things they don't like.

- Stay calm, quiet, and gentle, yet be firm at the same time.
- Stick to the regular routine; maybe include a book or quiet music.
- Make sure the bedroom is quiet with the lights dim or off.
- No food or drink in the bed or crib.
- Tuck the toddler in by putting them down and saying goodnight.

The child will sense if they can manipulate you.

Children might try to find excuses and stall when you are putting them down for a nap or bedtime. Because you are the babysitter and not their parents, they will try to get you to bend the rules. No matter what they try it is always still best to follow the parents' routine and schedule. Do not force the child, but you may need to keep repeating until it works.

Some toddlers will need a diaper change before and after nap or bedtime, and some who have already been potty trained may still wear a pull-up to bed.

Once the children are napping, it is important to stay awake and alert. Use the baby monitor or video monitor. This is a good time to tidy up, do homework, or watch TV. If you start to feel sleepy, splash some cold water on your face and drink a large glass of water.

Remember—you should bring friends or visitors unless you have asked the parents' permission first.

Ask the parents what to do if the toddler won't go down; you may have to tuck them in several times or gently rub their back until they fall asleep. This is normal, so don't worry. You can do it!

CRYING

Don't be alarmed when toddlers cry. Remember, their words are still developing and they can express themselves through shrieking or crying.

I like to say things like: "Do you feel sad? Well, you can have a big cry and we will talk when you are done."

Hurt, Attention, or Fake Crying?

There are differences between a "hurt" cry, "attention" cry, and "fake" crying. With a hurt cry, it could have been because they stubbed their toe or got their hand caught in a toy, which may need immediate, comfort, and reassurance. In this case, pick up the toddler and console them.

A toddler can start crying if they crave attention or want something now. A perfectly happy content child might start an attention cry if they want your attention. You can quickly and quietly say, "Put your tears away and use your words, please."

A fake cry might happen if a toddler wants you to do something, like read a book over and over. When you announce it's the end, they may try to force some tears and a scrunched up face to draw you in to change your mind. Try not to look shocked. Instead, say something like, "We can read that book again after your nap, mealtime, or after we tidy up." Then, keep going. Fake tears will usually subside once they realize you are not giving in.

In all cries, you can always say, "Do you need a hug?" then let them come to you; don't rush over to them. Crying is a normal stage for toddlers.

TANTRUMS

If the toddler has a tantrum (with crying, yelling, screaming, and throwing themselves on the ground), it is mostly for your benefit and to see what you will do for them to get them to stop.

Therefore, you should **not** try to stop the tantrum. The best thing you can do is to sit back and wait until they settle down. Don't yell, panic, or say anything. When they settle down, say something like, "You must feel sad; tell me what's wrong/why you're sad." Gently rub their back and redirect them by suggesting a new activity, like reading a book or playing a game. Always stay calm.

Never ever yell, shake, grab, or hit the child; just do your best to ride it out.

QUIET TIME

Toddlers' lives are full of bubbling energy; they can easily go from one toy to another. They are curious, busy, and often have a TV show like *Dora the Explorer* on. Every toy blings, sings, and lights up. However, too many toys can be overwhelming.

So, it's always a good idea to establish some peaceful quiet time. Ask the toddler to help you tidy up so the room isn't chaotic, or you can clean the place up yourself while they are napping. That way, there will be no distractions.

Here are seven quiet time activities for toddlers:

1. **Puzzles**—A fun puzzle with a few pieces on the floor can entertain a toddler for a long time.
2. **Painting or colouring**—A blank piece of white paper, some crayons or washable markers, or paint will keep a toddler quiet while also allowing them to exercise their creativity and imagination. Put them in their high chair with the safety belt on.
3. **Picture books**—Find about five or six picture books

and look at each page together. You can ask them some questions about the content, such as, "Where is the cow?" or "Where is the red ball?"

4. **Interactive books**—Interactive books, such as pop-up books, will allow them to not only look at colourful pictures, but also exercise other senses like touch.

5. **Building blocks**—Lego, wooden blocks, or cardboard bricks spread out on a clear empty floor can keep a toddler occupied for hours.

6. **Go for a walk**—Dress the toddler appropriately and strap them in their stroller if you decide to go for a thirty-minute walk. ***Make sure you have discussed this activity with the toddler's parents beforehand.*** The fresh air, birds, and sights will be a nice quiet time for both of you.

7. **Fridge magnets**—Even if they have outgrown baby toys, fridge magnets are always a hit and will quickly mesmerize toddlers for hours (make sure they are too big for the toddlers to fit in their mouths).

PLAYTIME

Playtime is serious business to toddlers because it's how they learn how the world works! In a way, play is "work" for a toddler.

Here are seven playtime activities for toddlers:

1. **Pretend Grocery Store**—Enjoy a game of pretend shopping. Use some of their toys, and you can also add some unopened light items from the kitchen, such as a little box of crackers.

2. **Playhouse**—You can make a fort out of pillows, blankets, and cushions; a teepee; or a cardboard house. Toddlers love any kind of playhouse. If you are using a cardboard box, let them colour it. Cut a window and door out. They will peek out and playhouse for hours.

3. **Stuffed Animal Fun**—Most toddlers have a ton of stuffed animals. Gather them all up and bring them to the playroom or couch. You can arrange them in various ways—all in a row, by colour, or make it look like they are having fun. If they have a dressable plush or animal doll, you can also dress and undress them in different outfits.

4. **Mailing letters**—Get some paper, crayons, and envelopes, then write some letters and draw pictures. Once you're done, seal them up and label them for Mom and Dad later. You and the toddler can also try colouring and drawing on the envelopes too.

5. **Make an indoor sandbox**—Fill a cardboard box with dried beans, rice, or oatmeal. Then, get some food containers and place the cardboard in the tub. Let the toddler play, scoop, and pour the "sand."

6. **Bowling with plastic water bottles**—Find some empty water bottles from the recycling that can be

used to play a game of bowling. Fill them half-way with water, rice, or beans to give them some weight, then set them up and roll a plastic ball toward them.

7. **Washing toys**—Fill a very small bowl with warm soapy water. Ask the toddler to bring out their toys, be it dolls, trucks, trains, among any others they may have. Set out a tea towel, then let the toddler wash their toys and place them on the tea towel to dry. Never leave a toddler alone with water and make sure to use a very tiny amount of water.

SET THE STAGE FOR SUCCESS

Good babysitters are safety-conscious, with safety always being first in their minds. Take extra precautions to make sure the children are safe. It doesn't matter how long you are babysitting for—if you are babysitting, your job is to focus on the kids at all times.

Toddlers are super busy and super curious; they lack a sense or understanding of danger, if they have any understanding of it at all. Therefore, you cannot be sure what they will do next. The best way to avoid trouble is to supervise and play with them the entire time you are babysitting.

THINGS TO WATCH OUT FOR

1. **Falls**: Toddlers are learning to walk and climb. Their

balance isn't that great yet, meaning they can be wobbly and step on a toy and fall down. They may try to push chairs or stools to a counter or table and climb up. There should be baby gates at the top and bottom of stairs, though some more agile toddlers can still crawl over them. Stay with them at all times to avoid a fall.

2. **Choking**: Like babies, toddlers can easily choke on food, toys, or household items. Hot dogs, batteries, and door stoppers are the most commonly choked on items. Cut their food up small and stay with them at all times to avoid choking hazards.

3. **Objects (in nose or ears)**: If the toddler doesn't try to put it in their mouth, they may try to jam a toy, food, or household object up their nose or ears. Watch them at all times to avoid this.

4. **Bumps and bruises**: Because toddlers don't anticipate danger, they can take some nasty falls. If a toddler trips or slips and falls, try to settle them down by comforting them.

5. **Poisoning**: Toddlers can quickly snatch up a bottle of vitamins or medicine and try to eat it. Toddlers may also put dishwasher tabs and laundry tabs in their mouths. Supervise them carefully and keep dangerous substances out of their reach.

6. **Drowning**: A toddler can drown within an inch of water, toilet bowl, or sink. We highly recommend not bathing a toddler when babysitting or taking

them swimming. If they have a pool, make sure the entry to the pool is closed off and locked. Never leave a toddler alone near water.

You must stay with toddlers at all times to ensure they are free from any danger or harm.

PRE-SCHOOLERS
(3 - 5 YEARS)

"To the **WORLD** you may be one person;
BUT to one person, **YOU** may be the world!"
- Dr. Seuss

THE **ULTIMATE** BABYSITTING COURSE

CHAPTER THREE: PRESCHOOL (3 - 5 YEARS)

Preschoolers are adorable. At this stage, they are preparing to go to preschool or a formal daycare, then kindergarten. They are developing the independence, vocabulary, and skills they will need to enter their school years.

Pros of babysitting preschoolers:

- More active
- Have fun activities to share together
- Are more capable at taking instructions

Cons of babysitting preschoolers:

- Activities can be more labor-intensive

PARENTAL EXPECTATIONS OF PRESCHOOLERS

A preschooler may do any of the following:

- Climb stairs well using both feet
- Kick balls
- Run easily
- Hop on one foot
- Pedal a tricycle
- Jump over objects
- Bend down to pick something up without falling
- Imitate adults, friends, TV characters
- Show love by hugging and kissing
- Learning to take turns in games
- Can dress alone (though may take some time)
- Brush teeth
- Hold a conversation (talk in sentences, ask questions, understand)
- Learn to use toilet
- Understands simple tasks such as, "Please clean up your toys"
- Listen well
- Match objects; can play matching games
- Learning numbers and how to count

VOCABULARY

The job of a toddler is to learn how to talk with basic words; the job of a preschooler is to learn more about grammar and how to piece words together so they can communicate through coherent sentences. They learn through imitating examples in their life.

Vocabulary development varies between each child. Preschoolers learn new words every day.

At three years old, most toddlers have a vocabulary of about 900 - 1000 words. At four years old, a preschooler can have 1500 - 2100 words in their arsenal.

By Age 3:

- Understand who, what, where, why
- Create sentences using five words or more
- Talk about past events like, "When they went to the park"
- Tell simple stories
- Enjoy rhymes and songs
- Know most of the alphabet
- Understand simple tasks with two steps

By Age 4:

- Follow simple directions
- Tell clear stories with a beginning, middle, and end
- Try to solve problems
- Match things together

- Learn numbers and letters
- Know most of the alphabet
- Talk easily and speak clearly

It's fun to babysit preschoolers because you can talk and communicate with them a lot better than when they were babies and toddlers.

Tips to Speaking to Preschoolers:

- Speak in a slow, clear, and simple manner.
- Make the conversation two-way—ask a question and listen for an answer.
- Ask questions that have a choice: "Would you like a red or yellow cup?"
- Read a book, then ask questions about the story: "Where is the barn?" and "What color is the horse?" for example.
- Have the preschooler do their best to read the story back to you. This is fun and they may try to improvise, looking at the pictures and remembering what you said.

HOLDING

A part of normal child development is becoming independent. Preschoolers do not need to be carried everywhere. An average preschooler weighs 30-40lbs. and can walk.

A better option to carry around a 3- to 5-year-old is to offer to hold their hand.

POTTY TRAINING AND TOILET ROUTINES

The preschoolers you are babysitting will most likely be using a toilet or a small "potty" now. Ask the parents what stage they are in potty training, their toilet routine, and stay consistent with the parents' potty training routine.

Beyond what the parents tell you, you should also notice for yourself what stage of potty training the preschooler is in. For example, if they are just learning to use the potty, they may wear a diaper or pull-ups. If they are starting to get the hang of it, they could be wearing underwear.

Most preschoolers in potty training still wear pull-ups to naptime or bedtime.

TIPS WHEN IT COMES TO POTTY TRAINING

- Ask the parents for specific instructions and follow them.
- Remind and encourage kids to use the potty every hour.
- Encourage preschoolers to use the potty before you go out.
- Before and after meals.
- Before and after naptime.

Rather than saying, "Do you need to use the potty?" (most likely a reply of no), say, "It's time to use the potty." Kids can't always tell when they need to go, so watch for signs, like the pee dance when they shift from foot to foot.

Lots of kids poop at regular times, such as after lunch. Ask the parents if their child normally has a bowel movement at a certain time of the day.

Don't get upset or make a fuss if there is an accident. Stay calm, change the child into clean clothes, then clean up the mess. Put the soiled clothing in the laundry. Accidents are a normal part of the training process.

Some parents use a reward system like stickers or Smarties™:

- ✓ Sticker or 1 Smartie for a pee

- ✓ Stickers or 2 Smarties for a poop.

Stick to the parents' routine.

DRESSING

Learning to dress and undress is an essential life tool, and most preschoolers enjoy dressing themselves. Learning to dress teaches fine motor skills (like using buttons and zippers) along with independence.

Let them choose their own outfits. Don't worry if they don't match—your job is just to make sure it's an appropriate choice. For example, you can't let them put on shorts in the middle of winter.

Be patient because it might take awhile. Don't criticize them, as learning to dress can be a challenge. Don't say things like, "You did it wrong; the buttons don't go that way," or "Your shirt is on backwards."

Instead, be positive. When they are done, say, "Great job. You look nice!"

FEEDING

Eating with a preschooler can be a lot of fun. Preschoolers are more cooperative than toddlers when it comes to food. Preschoolers can feed themselves using a spoon and fork. I don't recommend letting them use a knife while you are babysitting.

Most preschoolers eat in a booster seat—make sure they are seated comfortably with the safety strap buckled up. Push their chair in close to the table so they can reach their food easily .

Always be cautious about foods that cause choking and cut them up before serving.

Foods that can cause choking:

- Slippery food such as grapes, meat, hot dogs, and candy
- Small hand food like nuts, popcorn, chips, raw carrots, and raisins
- Sticky foods like marshmallows, peanut butter, and granola bars

Always cut food up in small pieces. You can make it fun by playing a counting game. Say, "Let's count how many grapes you have while you eat them." Set a good example by sitting and eating with the preschooler.

Questions to ask the parents:

Ask the parents what they would like you to feed their preschooler. Also, ask if there are any food allergies; if there are any forbidden foods not allowed and what time to feed the children. How would they like it prepared?

Remember, preschoolers can eat with forks and spoons, though they still also like using their hands.

WHAT TO FEED

- 3 - 5 years
- Whole milk
- Cheese
- Yogurt

- Fruits—fresh fruit (cut up small) oranges, apples, grapes, watermelon, pineapple, cantaloupe, bananas
- Vegetables—celery, carrots, cucumber, red and yellow or green beans, sugar snap peas, broccoli, cauliflower (cut small)
- Protein*—1 slice of toast & peanut butter, 4 - 6 crackers, hard boiled eggs, scrambled eggs, ½ cup cooked rice, pasta, cereal

Remember to always check with the parents in terms of peanut butter, eggs, and peanut protein. Make sure that the parents have already introduced these foods and whether they are okay with serving them. If you are unsure, don't serve them.

SAFETY TIPS

- Sit with the children and watch as they eat. Don't take your eyes off them. This way, you can see what they are putting in their mouths. Make sure the child is always sitting when they are eating to avoid choking.
- Make sure they are buckled into their booster chair and pulled up to the table.
- Don't let them use knives.
- Don't coax or beg them to eat. The more you push them, the more they will refuse. Instead, eat your

meal and look like you are enjoying your food! The child will become more likely to eat if you eat with them and not merely sit and stare at them.

- Keep a written chart for the parents and write down everything they eat.
- If you microwave any of the food, taste it first to ensure it's not too hot.
- Check with the parents regarding what their child can drink (water, juice, or milk) and when to serve it.
- I only serve water between meals and snacks, so the children don't fill up on juice.
- Model good table manners.

PRESCHOOLERS AND SLEEP

Preschoolers need about 11 - 12 hours of sleep every 24 hours, which will most likely include a nap.

SLEEP CHART GUIDELINE

Age	Night Time Sleep	Naps	Total
3-5 YEARS	10-11 HOURS	1-2 HOURS	11-12 HOURS

SLEEPING TIPS:

It is important to stay consistent with the parents regarding the preschooler's bedtime/naptime. Sleep experts say that children with an orderly bedtime and naptime routine sleep well and have a healthy brain development as a result.

There are many benefits to a bedtime routine:

- The prediction of a routine keeps the preschooler feeling safe and secure.
- A well-rested preschooler will most likely have a happy disposition.
- Have a down period before bed and let them know in advance that "In fifteen minutes, we will start getting ready for bed/a nap."
- Avoid horseplay and winding them up before bed/their nap.
- Let the preschooler pick out the pj's to wear and get them interested in going to bed.
- Remind them to use the potty before bed/naptime.
- Remember to put on a pull-up if they sleep in one.
- If they have an accident in bed, don't fret. Change them into dry clean pj's or clothing and remove soiled items and put in the laundry room.
- When a child is calm and relaxed, tuck them in snuggly and rub their back for a minute, saying "Good night."

If they put up a fuss, stay calm and firm, then repeat the process.

Once the child is napping, stay awake and alert. Use the baby video monitor. Check them every fifteen to twenty minutes.

This is a good time to gather and tidy up, and do homework or read.

Remember: no visitors or friends allowed unless you have permission from the parents first.

CRYING PRESCHOOLERS

A preschooler will most likely not cry as easily as a toddler or baby. Preschoolers can talk and communicate to you to tell you what's wrong.

Crying is a signal to tell you that something wrong or a need is not being met. Ignoring a cry is like ignoring a smoke alarm, since crying is meant to get your attention.

- Give the child a hug. Calm them down and ask what's wrong.
- Preschoolers can have separation anxiety when their parents leave; this is a completely normal reaction.
- Separation anxiety is a normal stage in the child's learning development; they love their mommy and daddy and don't understand why they are going away, or if/when they will return.

When a child is crying, they are usually worried about the parent leaving.

Here's what to do to console a crying preschooler:

- Soothe them for as long as it takes.
- Once they settle down, re-direct their attention to something else like a toy, activity, or games.
- Be honest if they ask, "Where is mommy?" Let them know that "Mommy went shopping. She will be home after your nap."
- This establishes trust between you and the child. By saying "after your nap," it gives them a sense of time because they most likely won't understand specific time, such as "3:00 o'clock."
- You should keep in mind the schedule. A child who is tired or hungry—if it's nearing time to eat—might cry more, louder, or longer than a content child.
- As you babysit this child more regularly, they will start to get used to the scene of mommy/daddy leaving.

Crying is normal.

You can handle it!

1. **Journal time**—Have the child jot down a couple words and draw a picture about what you did together that day.

2. **Colouring popsicle sticks**—Have the preschooler colour popsicle sticks in different colours, then match them up.

3. **Practice spotting the word**—Read a book and, after each page, ask the preschooler to point out a specific word, such as "the" or "at," then count how many times you saw it.

4. **UNO**—Use Uno cards to play a memory match game. Pull out seven sets of matching cards. Turn them over and take turns finding matches.

5. **Colouring**—Good old-fashioned colouring books!

6. **Teddy bear picnic**—Pop down a towel or tablecloth on the floor. Then, up a tea party and bring out familiar dolls, stuffed animals, or any other toys the preschooler thinks should participate.

7. **Screen time**—Let them use an iPad or an electronic game for a specific amount of time. Try to limit the use to educational games only.

PLAYTIME

Preschoolers are a lot of fun! When it's playtime, they don't fool around. Preschoolers talk well and are excited about life and each new adventure. If they are in a daycare or a play-group, they are making new friends. Preschoolers have wonderful imaginations and love to play, period.

Here are some activities you can do with a preschooler, as long as you have checked with mom and dad that they are okay.

1. **Build-a-Train**—You will need several cardboard boxes, large enough for the preschooler to sit in. Paper plates make the wheels, while markers, crayons, and stickers will decorate your train. Make sure you also have a cute conductors hat. Once the train is decorated, arrange the boxes in a "train" by pushing them together. Let the toddler sit inside and go on an imaginary choo-choo ride. *All aboard!*

2. **Happy, silly, sad, mad, sick, CUTE FACE GAME**—You will need six or seven pieces of square paper. On each piece of paper, draw a different face with a different expression: happy, silly, sad, mad, sick, cute. Put the papers face down on the floor. Ask the child to pick up a "face" and act out the feeling on the face. Get ready to laugh; this is a fun game!

3. **Hot or Cold Game**—What you need: an object, like a ball, toy, or anything small. How to play:

4. Choose one child to be the "finder."

5. Send him out of the room to count to 25 slowly.

6. Hide the object.

7. Ask the finder to come back in the room and look for an object.

8. Shout out hints as they get nearer the object, saying

"hot, hot, hot," or when they are getting away from the object, saying "cold, cold, cold."

9. Play until the object is found. Take turns; let the child hide the object while you go out of the room.

10. **I Spy**—How to play:

11. Take turns spotting objects within your eyesight.

12. Give out descriptive hints: "I spy with my little eye… something that is green."

13. The child gets to guess what the object is. For example: is it a plant? Is it my shirt? Is it broccoli? Once the child guesses right, they get to be the next "spy."

14. **Mother May I?**—How to play:

15. Have the child stand about 15ft. away from you and facing you.

16. Give directions and say, "Take one step forward."

17. The child has to say, "Mother, may I?"

18. You would say yes or no.

19. The child would then say, "Thank you" before taking the one step forward.

20. Play until the child reaches you, then switch places.

21. **My Favourite Things game**—You will need paper, pencils, and crayons. Ask the child to tell you all their favourite things, such as ice cream cones, dogs, mom, and dad. As they tell you, print out the name, *ice cream*; then, draw the picture. See how long you can make the list!!

22. **Play the Tidy-Up Game**—Reward the child for

tidying up by letting them pick an activity for you to do together.

SET THE STAGE FOR SUCCESS:

Preschool SAFETY TIPS

- Stay focused and safe when babysitting a preschooler.
- Preschoolers are busy and noisy, and it's amazing how much mischief they can get into on their own. Therefore, it's important to keep a watchful eye on them at all times.
- If you can't see the preschooler and everything has gone quiet, that likely means trouble. Check on them right away.
- You need to be clear on the parents' rules. Preschoolers may tell you they are allowed to do certain things, or say, "Mommy always lets me watch TV and cut with scissors."
- Taking care of children is the most important job *in the world!*

If you know the rules and they ask you to do something you don't feel comfortable with, or that you think isn't 100% safe, then say *NO*. Then, redirect them to another activity.

DANGERS TO WATCH OUT FOR

Falls—Preschoolers can climb, and generally have no fear. In the blink of an eye, they can be on top of the dresser or the refrigerator. A preschooler can get hurt if they fall off something high or low, and they can even break an arm or leg.

Poisoning—A preschooler can try to act like a grown-up and take a bottle of pills like aspirin, Tylenol, or children's vitamins. Make sure dangerous chemicals, medications, and household cleaners are out of reach. If you suspect poisoning, call the poison control centre right away.

Poison Control number: _____

Drowning—Preschoolers may love water, but it is never a good idea to let them swim, or for you to bath them while babysitting. A preschooler could drown in just a few inches of water.

Choking—Just like babies and toddlers, preschoolers will slip just about anything in their mouth: marbles, toy cars, barrettes, pen lids, paper clips, and, of course, food. Any of these could choke them. Supervise them carefully and always tell them, "Only put food in your mouth, please."

Safety is always first.

The best way to keep them safe is to stay with them at all times. Supervise them and keep your eyes on them.

SCHOOL AGE
(5 + YEARS)

You can find magic
wherever
you LOOK.
Sit back & relax,
all you need is
a book.

- Dr. Seuss

CHAPTER FOUR: SCHOOL-AGED CHILDREN (5 YEARS AND UP)

*S*chool-aged children are a lot of fun to babysit. They admire teenagers and will be excited to socialize with you. They will have lots of questions for you and about everything!

The Benefits of Babysitting School-Aged Children

- They understand rules and routines.
- They are independent and can do most things on their own (with supervision by you, of course).
- They will have developed their own personality and will have specific likes and dislikes.
- They can play or read independently, which allows you some time to care for other siblings or tidy up.

Vocabulary to Use with School-Aged Children

School-aged children around five years of age or older have language skills that are developing very quickly. These children use complete sentences, and they can read and write. These children also have a longer attention span than preschoolers, and they ask clear, logical sentences.

School-aged children are learning how to problem solve, listen, and answer questions that are relevant to the situation. They like to tattletale and want to please you. They like your approval, so they get excited when you call them a good girl or good boy, or say "Great job!" to them.

By the time a child reaches school age and enters kindergarten, they will have between a 2100 - 2200 word vocabulary. A six-year-old in grade one who typically has a 2600-word speaking vocabulary, can understand 20,000 - 24,000 words. By the time they turn twelve years old, they will understand around 50,000 words or more, which is incredible!

Why is vocabulary important?

Vocabulary is the basis for learning language, reading, and communicating.

How to encourage vocabulary development:

Read with the child you babysit, and have them read to you.

MEAL TIMES

Children will need to eat well throughout the day to ensure they are happy, healthy, and nourished. Children who eat well behave better and have more energy to play.

It can be tempting to eat things that are quick, full of sugar, and just not good for us. Set a good example for the school-aged kids you are babysitting by sitting and eating with them. That also means, of course, to try eating mostly or exclusively healthy snacks. The parents will most likely give you a list of what to feed the children for mealtimes and snacks.

Remember to relax and have fun. There is no reason to be in a hurry. Sitting and eating together should be an enjoyable and a fun way to connect and socialize with the child you are babysitting.

Healthy Snacks

Snacks play an integral role in managing kids' hunger and

boosting their nutrition. This does not mean that a school-aged child should eat a cupcake every half hour—the key word is "healthy."

Snacks can keep children from getting too hungry and cranky.

Here is a good list of simple snacks:

- Cereal
- Fruit
- Crackers and cheese
- Apple and peanut butter, if no food allergies
- Applesauce
- Banana
- Granola bars
- Yogurt
- Raw veggies and dip
- Hard boiled eggs

If you are feeding the school-aged children lunch or dinner, the parents should leave you instructions on what to feed them. If they don't, then ask. If it's left up to you, here are some ideas:

- Tuna sandwich and vegetable soup
- Pasta
- Rice with corn and peas
- Leftovers, like spaghetti or lasagna

- Frozen pizza & veggies and dip

SLEEP

Five- to six-year-olds need 10 - 12 hours of sleep per night. Children at this age go to bed between 8:00 and 9:00 and wake up at around 7:00 or 8:00 a.m. Most five-year-olds will not be taking afternoon naps.

Seven- to twelve-year-olds need to sleep 10 - 11 hours per night. As the children get older and have activities like swimming lessons, dance, and hockey, they tend to go to bed a bit later, which would usually end up being around 9:00.

As a side note, twelve- to eighteen-year-olds need to sleep about 8 to 10 hours per night. This is most likely the category that you fall into! Sleep is an important part of development for the health and well-being of teenagers. Some teenagers sleep longer—up to twelve hours on a weekend!

Adequate sleep makes you feel better and is a key ingredient to living a healthy lifestyle.

Here are some benefits of sleep:

- Improved memory
- Live longer
- Inspires creativity
- Improves athletic performance
- Improves grades in school
- Better attention span

- Happier and more fun to be around
- Increases brain power
- The right amount of beauty sleep can help you look and feel better

Sleep is as important as food and water. Proper sleep can also keep you from getting sick.

Everything that's alive needs sleep. Hopefully, the child you're babysitting and yourself have had enough sleep!

PLAYTIME

It doesn't take much to spark a school-aged child's imagination. Here are some ideas to play with school-aged kids while babysitting.

1. **Simon Says**—Choose one person to call out actions to the children. Whenever the caller says, "Simon Says," everyone must do the action. For example, if Simon says to "jump up and down," everyone must jump up and down. "Simon says, touch your nose," "Simon says, balance on one foot," and "Simon says lay down and pretend to sleep" are some good examples to get you started. If the caller doesn't start by saying, "Simon Says," no one should do the action, and if someone does the action, they are out!

2. **Junior Master Chef**—Kids love being in the kitchen,

so let them help you make a snack, lunch, or dinner. Get them to write down the recipe and steps on a piece of paper, then come up with a name for the creation.

3. **Talent Show**—This is a great way to get the imagination fired up. Get the kids to perform a well-known song or dance, or you can even make one up! You could also choose one of their favourite TV shows, and they can act out their own episode. Be sure to demonstrate for them first!

4. **Search for the Button (or object)**—For this game, you will need a button or small object. Everyone leaves the room except for the button hider. The hider would then hide the button somewhere unexpected. When the kids return to the room, they would search for it. Once a player spots the button, they must sit quietly without giving up the secret location of the button. The last child still searching for the button loses the game. Take turns!

5. **Music Band**—For this activity, you will need pots, pans, non-glass bowls, and some wooden spoons. You don't need expensive instruments to make fabulous music. Play some music and let the kids use the pots and pans to make music and play along.

6. **Dressing Up**—For this activity, you will need some old clothes, hats, mitts, and shoes. You should bring your own little box of old clothes and Halloween costumes, then let the kids have fun dressing up.

Snap some photographs, create a catwalk, and have a fashion show!

7. **Child's Turn**—Let the kids teach you how to play with their toys! Let them choose a game, toy, or activity to do; it's their turn to be the teacher. Smile, have fun, show interest, and give compliments. "That was a great idea!" and "I never thought of that!" will help encourage them during playtime.

All kids are different; some like energetic play and some are a little more reserved. No matter their disposition, don't rush the kids. Let them problem solve and encourage them to use their imaginations. Remember to tidy up after playtime, so the parents won't mind the fun time you've had.

QUIET TIME

It can be hard for kids to understand the importance of quiet time. You can set the stage for success in any situation and get school-aged kids to engage in some quiet time. Thirty minutes of quiet time is good for both the child and yourself.

Here are some quiet games and activities to keep the kids occupied and quietly entertained without putting them in front of the TV.

1. **Tic Tac Toe**—If you are babysitting more than one child, you can give them paper and pencils and show

them how to play Tic Tac Toe. Let them keep score quietly and ask them to play twenty games.

2. **Puzzles**—Keep some interesting puzzles in your babysitter kit. Set the child up at the kitchen table to quietly complete the puzzle.

3. **Reading**—School-aged children love to read. Keep a copy of Judy Blume's *Tales of a Fourth Grade Nothing* and *Blubber*, and Dr. Seuss's *Cat in the Hat* in your babysitting kit!

4. **UNO**—Uno can be played quietly with two or more players. Keep a deck of UNO cards in your babysitter's kit. If there is just one child, encourage them to play a memory game. Take out matching pairs of identical cards, then lay them out on the floor and let the child play memory.

5. **Beading**—All kids will enjoy beading. Put out assorted beads (from the dollar store) and some pre-cut yarn, then let the child make jewellery.

6. **Writing letters**—Encourage the kids to write a handwritten letter to their grandparents, aunts, uncles, or best friend. Help them seal up an envelope and give to mom and dad to address the envelopes. Pick up some letterheads and stickers.

7. **Write a booklet the children write and illustrate their own book**—You can have them quietly read it to you once they are finished.

SET THE STAGE FOR SUCCESS: SAFETY FOR SCHOOL-AGED CHILDREN

The school-aged child you are babysitting will most likely know their parents' household rules. They can show confidence and independence and may say, "Mom and Dad let me bike to the park all by myself, every day." Unless you have explicit permission from the parents, do not allow anything you are uncomfortable with. If they are adamant, you can always say, "Okay, let's call your mom and dad and ask." That should put an end to it, or you will gain permission from their parents if what they say is true.

Safety for School-Aged Children:

Burns—Don't let a school-aged child cook, use the stove or microwave, the dishwasher, or lighters.

Outdoor safety—Dress appropriately and supervise closely.

Car safety—Do not let the child you are babysitting play near the road or near cars at all.

Bicycle injuries—The child most likely has a bike and knows how to use it. Ask the parents for specific rules regarding biking and always insist on the child wearing a bicycle helmet.

Drowning—Never take a child you are babysitting swimming in a lake, pond, or pool. Drowning happens way too quickly. Even if the child has taken lessons and knows how to swim, the answer should still be no. If they wish to swim, they have to wait for their parents to return home first. Suggest running through a backyard sprinkler instead.

Use your instincts when babysitting a school-aged child. It is your responsibility to keep them safe and well taken care of. If you don't feel comfortable with something, redirect them to another activity.

Safety Tips For Babysitters

CHAPTER FIVE: SAFETY TIPS FOR BABYSITTERS

Good babysitters are safety-conscious and take extra care and attention to make sure that the children and themselves are safe and secure from harm. Home is where most children under ten get hurt. The main concerns for child safety at home are fire, falling, choking, poisoning, suffocating, and drowning.

The children should always be your main focus. Never take your eyes off them while they are in your care.

The following sections will outline tips for keeping key areas *safe*.

THE KITCHEN

- When cooking, use the back burners so the child

doesn't reach up and touch the hot surface.

- Turn pan handles inward so the child doesn't walk by and grab or bump the handle, spilling hot or scalding food on themselves.
- Keep the children away from the stove, oven, toaster oven, kettle, and microwave.
- Keep hot drinks, such as hot chocolate or tea, away from the children.
- Electrical outlets should have a safety plug in them.
- Keep all the sharp objects like knives, scissors, can openers, out of reach and out of sight.
- Keep the cleaning products' cupboard closed.
- Make sure vitamins and medications are out of reach, out of sight, and sealed up.

THE TELEPHONE

- If you answer a phone call, don't take your eyes off the children.
- Don't tell the caller that you are home alone babysitting; instead say that the parent is busy right now and ask to take a message. If the caller becomes bossy, inappropriate, or demanding, hang up and call the police.

ANSWERING THE DOOR

If the doorbell rings, take caution when opening the door. Ask who it is before opening the door. If you don't recognize the name or the parents never mentioned a visitor, do not open the door. If they seem persistent, call the police immediately. If it's a child's friend, know the rules in advance for having friends over.

Children have a habit of running to the door to see who is there. It is a game for them, especially in a house with multiple young ones. This habit can allow unwanted elements into the house. If you are not expecting a visitor and do not recognize the person at the door, do *not* open the door. If they say they have a message for you or one of the kids, call the emergency contact number and confirm the same from the parents. Also, ask the parents to curtail this habit in their children, so it is not a discipline issue for you while you babysit them.

While indoors, close and bolt all the doors and windows, and keep all entrances and exits clear of clutter.

OUTDOOR SAFETY

- Children can be unaware of the dangers when playing outside.
- Constantly supervise the children when outside; do not take your eyes off them.
- Make sure you know the parents' rules in advance before playing outside.
- Set clear boundaries—for example, tell the kids that

they can play in the backyard for twenty minutes,
then let them know you all are going back inside.

- If you have to cross the road, insist that the children
hold your hand.
- Check for sharp objects and broken glass on the
ground.
- Watch out for stray dogs.
- Be aware of any strangers nearby.
- Make sure the kids are dressed properly (i.e. a hat or
jacket in the colder weather).
- Bring bottled water, band-aids, and tissues with you.

BICYCLE SAFETY

Cycling is great fun and good exercise; however, caution and
safety is still your priority.

- If the kids are allowed to bike, make sure they are
wearing a helmet. Be a good example by wearing a
helmet too.
- Set clear boundaries about how far they can bike. For
example, you can tell them, "You can bike three
houses down the sidewalk, and three houses back."
- Ask the parents what their rules are around bike
riding and follow them closely.
- Use a bike lane if your city has one.
- Always ride close to the curbs.
- Stop and look both ways before crossing a road.
- Teach the kids to make eye contact with the drivers;

that way, you will know for sure that the driver sees you.

- No night time bike riding. Drivers cannot see you late at night.

The most important part of riding a bike is learning how to do it safely.

FIRE SAFETY

- Make sure you have walked through the entire house you are babysitting at.
- Know where the fire exits are and have a plan to meet the kids outside at a certain place.
- If a fire breaks out, it can spread very quickly. Get the kids and yourself out immediately.
- Call 911 from a neighbour's house.
- Never go back into the house to get something.
- If you are upstairs and cannot get downstairs, go to the furthest room away from the fire. Shut the door and try to get out a window.
- Close all the doors between you and the fire.
- If a door is hot, do not open it.
- If a fire breaks out on the stove, get the children and get out.
- If you or a child catches on fire remember: **STOP**

DROP + ROLL to put the flames out. Don't run and get the clothes off if possible.

FIRE SAFETY (FOR THE BABYSITTER)

Be responsible. Babysitting is a huge responsibility, and you should always keep a watchful eye on the children.

Make sure you have an exit plan. Every house should have one, and you can discuss this with the parents before they leave. Make sure you are familiar with the house and know where all the exits, doors, and windows are. Establish a meeting place outside where everyone should meet in case a fire breaks out.

Put away all matches and lighters. Out of sight, out of reach of the kids, and out of the kids' minds. Never smoke while babysitting (*or ever!*)

Be safe in the kitchen. Only cook if the parents have given you permission and instructions. Never leave anything cooking on the stove unattended. Turn the handles of the pots and pans inward so a child doesn't reach up and grab it. Use the rear burners.

Be safe. Check to see if fire alarms are installed on each floor. Most have a green light that indicates they are working.

WHAT TO DO IF THERE IS A FIRE

- Don't panic.
- Get everyone out of the house and stay out.
- If there is smoke, crawl on the floor under the smoke. Smoke rises, and there may be some cleaner air nearer the ground. Do *not* inhale the smoke.
- Call 911 from a neighbour's house.
- Watch the children carefully until the fire department and the parents arrive.

WATER

Drowning is the leading cause of death and injury of children. Seconds save lives.

If the family you babysit has a pool, hot tub, or wants you to bathe the kids or has told you it's okay to take the kids swimming, I strongly urge you not to take on this responsibility, no matter how well the kids or you can swim. It is not worth the risk.

As a graduate of The Babysitter Club, I want you to make it known to the parents of the kids you are watching that you will not be taking them swimming or bathing them. Tell them that you are not comfortable with this.

If the family you are babysitting has a pool or hot tub, make sure any door leading out to the pool is locked. Most families will also usually have a chain lock on the top of the door that is locked, which the kids can't reach.

Indoor pools are even more dangerous. If the family for

which you are babysitting has an indoor pool, make sure it is locked up.

Play pools can also be just as dangerous as a full-sized pool or hot tub. Kids can drown in as little as an inch or two of water. There are too many tragic stories about kids drowning every year.

If it's fall or winter, and the pool is closed for the season, it can be just as dangerous as when it's open. This is true even with safety covers on top. If a child tries to walk on the safety cover, it can collapse and suck the child down, trapping and drowning them.

Babysitting at a house with a pool is an even bigger responsibility. If you don't feel comfortable, then follow your gut instinct and turn the job down. It is not worth the few extra bucks. The parents will also be glad you were honest and they will understand.

Even toilets are drowning hazards. Remember that children can drown in as little as one or two inches of water. Keep the toilet lids down and wait outside the door when kids are using the bathroom. Make sure the kids know that a toilet is not a toy. If a child falls into the toilet head first, they won't be able to get out. There have been tragic cases in which kids have drowned in toilets. Some parents will have a safety latch on their toilet. Do not let children lock the bathroom door while using it.

Toilets can be overlooked as a drowning hazard. Kids are

naturally drawn to water, so you need to stay one step ahead of them and keep those toilet lids closed.

HOW TO HANDLE EMERGENCIES

Preparing in Advance for Emergency Situations

Most babysitting jobs go very smoothly. The most important aspect of babysitting is to make sure the children and your-self are safe and secure. Read this section every time before you babysit to ensure you are prepared in case an emergency situation happens.

Emergency Contact Information

Remember to have the parents fill out the Emergency Contact Information Sheet provided in this book before they leave. There is a pad included in your babysitter kit. If you run out, you can order another pad online at www.the-babysittingclub.com.

The sample Emergency Contact Information Sheet can be found in the Introduction chapter of this book.

This is not a first-aid course. It is highly recommended that you take a basic CPR and first aid course before you start babysitting. Call the Canadian or American Red Cross, YMCA, and/or St. John's Ambulance. All the information in this section has been obtained from the Canadian Red Cross website. Again, this does not replace a CPR or first aid course.

WHAT IS 911?

The number 911 is the universal emergency number for everyone in the United States and Canada. According to the National Emergency Number Association (NENA) over 150 million calls are made to 911 each year.

911 is an easy number to remember that will give you access to all emergency services, including:

- Fire
- Police
- Ambulance

What to Expect When You Call 911

When you call 911, use your emergency sheet. Stay calm and answer questions in a clear voice for the 911 dispatcher.

The 911 operator/dispatcher, will ask you for the following information:

- Do you need fire, ambulance, or police?

- The location and address of the emergency
- A description of what is happening
- Your name, address, and telephone number
- The apartment or access code, if applicable

Let the operator ask the questions. They are trained to ask you questions in a specific order to help you as quickly as possible.

Follow their instructions and do not hang up. After the call is completed, they may ask you to remain on the line. If anything else happens, it will be better to have them right there on the line.

Things to Do While Waiting for Emergency Workers to Arrive

- Clear a path to the patient; they will bring a stretcher in. Move furniture out of the way and unlock the doors.
- If possible, have someone stand outside the door to wave the ambulance down when they arrive on your street.
- Turn the outdoor lights on.
- If you are in an apartment, try to get a neighbour to

meet the ambulance workers in the lobby.

- Do not move the patient.
- Sit with the patient and hold their hand. Speak calmly and tell them help is on the way and everything is going to be okay.
- Pray with them.

When you call 911, you are the first part of the emergency medical service chain.

The emergency chain flows like this: You call 911, the 911 dispatcher calls fire, ambulance, and/or police on the way to help.

It might be scary to think about emergencies when babysitting; however, babysitting is a very great responsibility and every second counts in an emergency. By being alert and prepared in advance, you can react quickly and correctly in an emergency situation.

When to Call 911 (*taken directly from the Canadian Red Cross website*)

You should call 911 **IF** you see anyone who is:

- Unconscious
- Not breathing
- Having difficulty breathing
- Bleeding a lot
- Vomiting blood

- Has injected poison
- Is having a seizure, severe headaches, can't talk
- Broken bones
- Head or spine injuries

Use your common sense and moral compass!

ILLNESS

You should call the parents right away if the child you are babysitting appears sick or ill.

Signs of illness include:

- Uncontrollable crying for a long period
- Fever, burning up
- Having trouble breathing
- Vomiting
- Dizziness, limp, lethargy

CHOKING *(taken directly from the Canadian Red Cross Guide)*

Prevent Choking

- Careful, slow eating, and chewing
- No walking, laughing, running, or talking while eating
- Make sure objects like pen caps and coins are not in children's mouths

- Keep the children still while they have food in their hands and mouths
- Feed babies and young children soft foods in small pieces
- Stay with them while they eat
- Always check the environment to make sure no small toys or objects are near babies or children, specifically those who will put things in their mouths
- Keep young children away from balloons that can pop into small pieces and be easily inhaled and get stuck in the children's throats

CHOKING (CONSCIOUS) - FOR BABIES UP TO 1 YEAR

If you see the baby you are babysitting coughing or breathing forcefully, check the scene and the baby:

1. If the baby can breathe or cough, stay with them. Do not try to stop the baby from coughing and don't slap them on their back.
2. If the baby is making high pitched noises, wheezing, can no longer make a sound, or becomes too weak to cough, shout for help and send someone to call 911.

CARE

1. Hold the baby face down on your arm between your hand and your elbow. The baby's head should be lower than the body.

2. Hold the baby's jaw firmly. Rest your arm on your thigh.
3. With the heel of your hand, give five firm back blows between the shoulder blades.
4. If the baby is still choking, turn their face upon your thigh, with their head lower than the body. Hold the back of their head.
5. Imagine a line between the baby's nipples. Place two fingers on the centre of the breastbone, one finger-width below the imaginary line.
6. With your two fingers, push down five times (these are called chest thrusts). You should press down $\frac{1}{3}$ to $\frac{1}{2}$ the depth of the chest. Match your strength to the baby's size.
7. After five chest thrusts, do five more firm back blows.
8. Repeat the chest thrusts and back blows sequence until:
9. the object comes out.
10. the baby starts crying, breathing, or coughing forcefully.
11. the baby becomes unconscious.
12. If the baby becomes unconscious, call EMS/911 for help if you have not already called them.

CHOKING (CONSCIOUS) - FOR CHILDREN OVER ONE:

If you see the child you are babysitting coughing or breathing forcefully, you need to check on the child.

- Check the scene and the child.
- Help the child lean forward. Encourage him or her to cough. Stay with the child and do not slap them on the back.
- If the child's face is turning blue or they are making a whistling sound, definitely follow the next sections.

Call

1. Shout for help
2. Send someone to call EMS/911

Care

1. Stand behind the child (for a small child, you may need to kneel behind them) and provide support by placing one arm diagonally across the chest, then bend the child forward at the waist. Give five firm back blows between the shoulder blades with the heel of one hand.
2. If the object has not come out of the child's mouth, put your arms around the waist. Make a tight fist, then put your fist just above their belly button, with your thumb against the belly.
3. Put your other hand over your fist.
4. Press your fist into the child's belly with a quick inward and upward thrust. Do this five times.

5. Match your strength to the child's size. The smaller the child, the gentler your thrusts need to be.
6. After five abdominal thrusts, do five more firm back blows.
7. Repeat the cycle of abdominal thrusts and back blows until:
8. the object comes out.
9. the child starts breathing or coughing forcefully.
10. the child becomes unconscious.
11. If the child becomes unconscious, call EMS/ 911 for help if you have not already called them.

BLEEDING: CUTS AND WOUNDS

For a very serious cut with lots of bleeding, remember:

- Rest. Have the child lie down.
- Direct pressure. Use a clean cloth applied directly over the cut.
- Use disposable gloves whenever you may have to touch any body fluids.
- Check the scene and the child.

Care:

1. Hold a clean cloth firmly against the wound. Remember to wear disposable gloves.
2. Get help if there is a lot of bleeding. Call EMS/911.
3. Have the child lie down and stay still.

4. If the cloth you are using soaks through with blood, don't take it away; put another cloth over it.

5. Tie a bandage around the cloth. If the cut is on the child's neck, don't tie a bandage on, but hold the cloth firmly.

6. If the bleeding stops, make a sling or use bandages to keep the hand from moving.

7. If the skin below the wound tingles, is cold, or it's blue, the bandage is too tight. oosen it slightly. If colour or temperature does not improve call EMS/911.

8. Wash your hands as soon as possible.

INTERNAL BLEEDING

If the child you are babysitting falls off a play structure at the park, there is a chance they could have internal bleeding if they show any of these signs:

- Very thirsty
- Pain where they were hurt
- Yawning and gasping for air
- Faintness
- Red or black vomit
- Bright foamy blood coughed up
- Swelling where he or she was hurt

Do not lift the child's feet, give them anything to drink, or move them. In the case of moving them, don't do so if you think they have hurt their neck. If they are in a position that makes it difficult for them to breathe, however, you may have to move them.

1. If the child has a hard time breathing because they are bleeding from their nose, mouth, or ears, roll them onto their side.
2. Send someone to call EMS/911.

NOSE BLEEDS

If the child you are babysitting has a nose bleed:

1. Tell them to sit down, then try to get them to relax.
2. Tilt their head forward a little bit.
3. Pinch their nostrils firmly together.
4. Hold firmly for at least 10 minutes without letting go.
5. If the bleeding continues, get help right away.

IMPALED OBJECT

This means that an object has punctured into the skin and is still stuck there.

If the child you are babysitting has a piece of glass sticking out of their leg or arm, never remove/pull out the impaled object because doing so could cause severe bleeding.

1. Cut any clothing away from the object.
2. Put bulky bandages on around the object to keep it from moving.
3. Tie the bandages in place.
4. Get help right away and call EMS/911.

If the child has a splinter sticking out of their skin, it is probably okay to use tweezers to remove it. Pull out the splinter at the same angle that it went into the skin.

SCRAPES

This is when the child you are babysitting falls and scrapes their skin.

1. Wash the scrape with running water for five minutes.
2. Wash the skin around the scrape with soap and water. Rinse the soap off thoroughly.
3. Blot the scrape with a sterile gauze dressing from a first aid kit or the medicine cabinet.
4. Cover with a sterile bandage.

SPRAINS, STRAINS, AND FRACTURES

1. Check the scene and the baby or child.
2. Call EMS/911…
3. *If* you think the child has injured their head, neck, or back.

4. *If* the injury makes walking or breathing difficult.
5. *If* you think there are several injuries.

CARE

For common injuries, remember **RICE**:

Rest. Make the child as comfortable as possible.

Immobilize. Immobilizing the injury lessens the pain, prevents further damage, and reduces the risk of bleeding.

Cold. Cold reduces pain and swelling.

Elevate. Raising the injury reduces swelling.

Children can hurt their head from a fall of only 15 centimeters or 6 inches.

Signs of a head injury include:

- Headache
- Dizziness or disorientation
- Nausea or vomiting
- Loss of consciousness
- Bleeding or clear liquid from ear to nose

Signs of a neck and back injury are:

- Pain
- Loss of feeling
- Loss of strength

Signs of leg or arm injuries are:

- Pain
- Tenderness
- Swelling

A head injury could also mean a neck or back injury. Do not move the child unless they are in a dangerous place.

INJURY EXAMPLE

A child has fallen off a swing at the park and seems to be hurt.

Check

Check the scene and the child and check if they are conscious. Ask them if they are okay.

Call

If they don't answer, shout for help. Have someone call EMS/911; or, if you are alone, call yourself.

Care

1. If the child is not breathing, begin child CPR (if you are trained to do so).
2. If the child is breathing, but is unconscious, check

for blood, vomit, or noisy breathing. If there is none, don't move the child.

3. If you hear gurgling or noisy breathing or see the fluid from their nose or mouth, roll the child onto their side to help them breathe better. Let their upper arm and leg roll toward the ground in the recovery position. Try to move the child's body all at the same time so that the neck doesn't get twisted.

4. Check to see whether the child is wearing a medic alert bracelet or necklace (if they wear a medic alert bracelet or necklace, the parents should have told you).

POISON

Prevention

- Keep the children away from all medications, cleaning products, and poisonous plants. Consider all household or drugstore products potentially harmful, including multi-vitamins and headache and cold medication.
- Never call medicine "candy" to get the child to take it.
- Never store household products in food or drink containers.
- Make sure the Poison Control Centre number is near the telephone.

- Wear shoes outdoors and do not walk through high grass or bushes.

Check

Check the scene and the baby or child.

Call

If you suspect any type of poisoning, call the local Poison Control Centre

_____ (number) to get advice immediately. The telephone number(s) should be posted with the other emergency numbers.

Care

Care for life-threatening conditions first. Provide care according to instructions from the poison control centre or EMS/911.

There are various types of poisoning that can occur and that you should always be thinking about.

Inhaled poison:

Signs of inhaled poison include:

- Red sore eyes, nose, or throat
- Coughing, hard time breathing, dizziness
- Vomiting, seizures
- Bluish colour around the mouth or red face

- Unconsciousness

Poison on the skin:

Signs of poison on the skin include:

- Burning, itching, swelling, blisters
- A headache, fever

Swallowed poison:

Signs of a swallowed chemical include:

- Burning in the mouth, throat, or stomach
- Cramps, gagging, diarrhea, nausea, vomiting

Signs of a swallowed plant or drug include:

- Vomiting seizures
- Irregular pulse
- Drowsiness, having a hard time talking, lack of coordination
- Dizziness
- Rapid breathing

BURNS

Prevention

- Keep matches and lighters away from children and always supervise them.
- Do not hold a hot drink while carrying a baby or toddler. Keep hot drinks and food where children cannot reach them.
- Cook on the stove with the pot handles turned in. Use red burners, and keep children away from the stove area.
- Never put water on a grease fire.
- Do not spray aerosol cans near an open fire.
- Never use electrical appliances near water.
- Cover electrical outlets with childproof safety caps.
- Avoid the sun between 10:00 am and 3:00 pm (when it's most intense).
- Wear protective clothing from the sun (including hats).
- Use sunscreen.

Check

Check the scene and the child.

Call

Call EMS/911 for burns that:

- involve difficulty breathing
- cover more than one body part
- occur on the head, neck, hands, feet, or genitals
- result from chemicals, explosions, or electricity

- are deep (skin has blisters and looks brown
  or black)

CHEMICAL BURNS

In this scenario, the child you are babysitting has an area of red skin and is crying. You think the child might have played with some cleaning products.

1. Rinse the affected skin with cold water for fifteen minutes. Do not use ice. Use a shower or hose if you need to.
2. Take off any clothes that have chemicals on them while you are rinsing.
3. Cover the burned skin with a clean, dry, non-stick dressing.
4. Get help right away and call EMS/911.

HEAT BURNS

A child you are babysitting has been playing near a hot radiator and has burned their leg. Don't take off any clothing that may be stuck to the burn.

1. If there are blisters, leave them alone. Never put greasy ointments (butter, lotions, or creams) on burns.
2. Put the burned skin in cool water for at least fifteen minutes. Don't use ice.

3. Cover with a clean, dry, non-stick dressing.
4. Get help for burns that are more than 5 cm (2 inches) around and for burns that are blistered, white, or black. Call EMS/911 for all burns to the head, neck, feet, or genitals.

ELECTRICAL BURNS

You hear a sudden loud pop from the bedroom of a child you are babysitting. You see a lamp overturned. The child seems confused and their hand is burned. In addition, they are having difficulty breathing.

1. Make sure the area is safe and there is no further risk of shock.
2. Monitor the child's breathing.
3. Look for two burns: where the electrical current entered AND exited. They will often be on hands and feet.
4. Cover the burns with a clean, dry, non-stick dressing.
5. Call EMS/911 for help.

SPECIAL HEALTH REQUIREMENTS

You should find out if the children you are babysitting have any special health requirements. If they require any special health assistance, you will need to know how to avoid problems and what to do if the children get sick.

Allergies

One in five children in North America has some kind of allergy. The most common allergies are tree and grass pollens, dust, insect bites, food, medications.

Always ask the parents if the children you are caring for have allergies. Some children may carry an EpiPen® in a special kit. Find out what you should do to assist if there is a problem.

The child may have learned to take their own medication; however, you may need to know how to get it out or get it ready for them.

Signs of Allergic Reaction

- Rash, hives (pale red swellings) and itching
- Feeling of tightness in the chest and throat
- Swollen lips, face, ears, neck, and or tongue
- Whistling or wheezing noises when breathing, changes in voice
- Nausea and/or vomiting

Check

In this example, let's say the child you are babysitting ate a peanut, but they are allergic to nuts. The child is having trouble breathing, and their lips and eyes have begun to swell up. Administer the EpiPen® (if they have it) and call EMS/911.

Care

1. Help the child take any medication from the allergy kit (i.e., EpiPen®) or use their inhaler, as necessary. Ask "yes" or "no" questions so the child can nod answers.
2. Open a window for fresh air.
3. Keep the child as comfortable as possible.
4. Continue to monitor the child's breathing.

ASTHMA

Asthma is a serious breathing problem often brought on by something a child is allergic to. Find out what you should do if a child you are caring for has an asthma attack.

Ask the parents if the child has an inhaler. There is a blue one and a red one. Some use one, whereas some use both. In some cases, they may have a machine (nebulizer), so you should find out when and how it should be used.

Signs of an Asthma Attack

- Fast shallow breathing and coughing
- Child says they can't breathe
- Child is confused, afraid, or nervous
- Child is dizzy, feels numb, has tingly fingers and toes
- A whistling, wheezing noise when the child breathes out

Check

Check the scene and the child. You should know beforehand that the child you are babysitting has asthma. After a walk through the park, you notice they are wheezing a lot. Call EMS/911 for help.

Care

1. Help the child use the inhaler as necessary.
2. Open a window for fresh air.
3. Keep the child as comfortable as possible.
4. If breathing does not improve, call EMS/911 for help if you have not already called them.
5. Continue to monitor the child's breathing.

SEIZURES

Children with pre-existing conditions may have some scary episodes, including seizures. Before accepting a job in such a home environment, make sure you are conversant with what to do. Take a course or two in this area if necessary. Seizures may be caused by epilepsy or high fever, and they can cause the child to lose control over their body and its movements.

Having quick reflexes is part of the job description of a babysitter, and so is the ability to communicate to emergency medical staff about what transpired with the child. It is preferable to do first aid while you call emergency numbers to get an ambulance over to the house. Some babysitters with a medical background will be quite capable of helping the child, then driving to the hospital themselves. Most are not, however, so quickly calling for medical help is still a good option.

Seizures are among the more serious safety issues to look out for because, in the moments the seizure is occuring, the child can seriously hurt themselves even further.

Check

Check the scene and the child.

Call

Have someone else call EMS/911.

Care

1. Move any furniture that is in the way and can hurt the child. Don't try to stop or control their movements.
2. Protect their head by putting a cushion or some folded clothing under it.
3. If there is saliva, blood, or vomit in the child's mouth, roll them into the recovery position.
4. Don't put anything between the child's teeth; an object could obstruct the airway.
5. After the seizure, if the child is unconscious, roll them into the recovery position. Call EMS/911 for help.

6. If the child is conscious, they may be tired and seem confused. Stay with them and make sure you are reassuring them.
7. Call the parents or a neighbour whose number you've been given.

BEE STINGS

The child you are babysitting is playing in the backyard and is stung by a bee.

Check

Check the scene and the child. In this case, you could find a red swollen spot (and stinger) where the bee stung the child.

Call

Call EMS/911, especially if the child has a severe allergic reaction.

Care

1. If you can see the stinger, scrape it away from the skin with your fingernail or a stiff card. Don't use tweezers because you may squeeze more poison into the child.
2. Wash the bite with soap and water, then cover it to keep it clean.
3. Put a cold pack over the sting to reduce pain and swelling.

4. Watch the child for signs of an allergic reaction (difficulty breathing or a lot of swelling).

FIRST AID KIT

All homes should have a first aid kit. Ask the parents where their kit is, or bring your own so you can also take it on outings or to the park. Make sure the first aid kit is out of reach of the children.

Contents:

- Emergency numbers
- Small and large sterile gauze pads
- Adhesive tape
- Bandages to make a sling
- Adhesive bandages in assorted sizes
- Scissors
- Tweezers
- Safety pins
- Ice bag or chemical ice pack
- Flashlight with extra batteries in a separate bag
- Antiseptic wipes or soap
- Pencil and paper
- Emergency blanket
- Barrier devices (i.e. disposable gloves and pocket mask or face shield)
- Eye patches
- Thermometer

CONCLUSION

Congratulations on completing the Ultimate Babysitting Course!

You have learned a lot of valuable information throughout this course, including the qualities of an excellent babysitter and how to care for infants, toddlers, preschoolers, and school-aged kids.

You have also learned how to keep yourself and the children in your care safe, solve problems, and handle minor emergencies.

I recommend that you read your manual often and bring it with you to every babysitting job!

Also, please connect with other babysitters, ask questions, and keep up to date on babysitting tips by joining our Facebook page.

I wish you success and joy in all your babysitting adventures.

L.A. Hoekstra, Early Childhood Educator

DEFINITIONS

A

AIRWAY

The pathway through which air moves from the mouth and nose to lungs.

ALLERGY

A negative reaction of the body to food, bug bites, or medication.

ASTHMA

When air pathways narrow and cause trouble breathing. Most often used remedy is a blue or orange inhaler/puffer.

AMBULANCE

911 emergency vehicle that takes people to the hospital.

B

BABIES

Aged birth to twelve months.

BABYSITTER

Person who takes care and is in charge of a child or children when the parents are away.

C

CHECK, CALL, CARE

Three action steps to take in an emergency

- check the child
- call 911
- care for the child while waiting for ambulance

CHOKING

A 911 emergency when the airway is partially or fully blocked.

COLD ICE PACK

A block of ice in the freezer used to reduce swelling.

CONSCIOUS

When a person is awake and not fainted or passed out.

CUT

A break in a child's skin. Wrap and apply pressure to stop bleeding.

CONFIDENCE

Feeling certain about something.

D

DIAPER

A piece of material to absorb pee and poo from a baby or toddler.

DISPATCHER

A 911 emergency operator.

- They will ask questions: What is your emergency? What is your address?
- They will send an ambulance, police or fire truck.

DIVERSITY

The difference in people's backgrounds, ethnic culture, religions, etc.

E

EMERGENCY - 911

A problem that needs medical help right away because someone is injured.

ENVIRONMENT

Your surroundings.

EPI-PEN

A needle filled with medication fitted into a tube that looks like a pen. It is used to inject a drug in someone who is having a severe allergic reaction to something.

F

FIRST AID

The care you give to someone who is hurt. It is important to act quickly to save a life.

FIRST AID KIT

A small kit that includes band-aids.

FORMULA

A liquid given to babies from birth to twelve months in a bottle instead of breast milk.

H

HYGIENE & HEALTH

Keeping yourself clean and healthy by showering, brushing your teeth and hair, wearing deodorant, and clean clothing.

HONESTY

The quality of being honest, truthful, and telling all facts.

I

INTEGRITY

The quality of being honest and having a strong moral value. To always do the right thing in all circumstances.

L

LEADERSHIP

Being in charge of a situation by showing responsibility.

M

MEDICATION

A pill or liquid used for medical treatment (i.e. Tylenol, Advil, doctor's prescription).

MORAL COMPASS

A person's capability to judge what is right and wrong, and how they do the right thing in any situation.

N

NAUSEA

The yucky feeling before throwing up. Feeling sick to your stomach.

NOSEBLEED

When the nose starts bleeding. If nosebleeds continue, sit down and tilt the head forward. Pinch nostrils firmly and breathe through the mouth. Hold firm for ten minutes without letting go. Call parents and 911.

P

POISONING

Eating, drinking, or breathing in a toxic solid, liquid, or gas that can injure or kill.

POISON CONTROL CENTRE

1-800-268-9017.

A medical facility that can provide immediate, free advice over the telephone in case of exposure to a poisonous substance.

PRESCHOOLER

Ages three to five years.

PLAYTIME

Time for active play.

PROFESSIONAL

Being responsible, mature, calm, reliable, and skilled.

Q

QUIET TIME

Time set aside to play or read quietly.

R

RECOVERY POSITION

Lying on one's side with the face angled towards the ground. This position is used to keep the airway open in case of vomiting.

RESUME

A list of your job experiences, dates, abilities, and skills, like a babysitting license.

- A contact list of references.
- Your contact information.

RECEIVING BLANKET

A small, lightweight blanket used to wrap an infant.

ROLE MODEL

Someone who acts responsible and teaches others to do the same.

RULES AND ROUTINES

Written down list of what the parents say you can and cannot do, along with routines they want you to follow. If you are unsure about a certain activity, don't do it. These rules exist for safety purposes.

S

SCHOOL-AGED CHILDREN

Five years and older.

SEIZURE

Electrical problems in the brain make you shake out of control. Can be caused by epilepsy or poisoning, high fever, or a head injury. Call 911.

SEVERE BLEEDING

Bleeding that won't stop gushing out, even when a band-aid is on. Call 911.

SUPERVISING

Keeping a watchful eye on the children at all times.

SUCCESS

You have been tasked with caring for an infant or a child.

How do you know that you are having an impact on them as their babysitter? The answer is simple: the accomplishment of a task. Of course, you have to concede that this is a combined effort with the parents and teachers, but pat yourself on the back. You are part of the village that is growing this baby.

T

TODDLERS

A child between the ages of one to three years old.

TOILET TRAINING

Teaching a child to use the toilet instead of a diaper. A child is usually taught to use the toilet between two and five years. Ask parents the toilet routine.

TRUST

Believing in the honesty and reliability of someone to do their best.

TRUTH

To always say exactly what happened.

U

UNCONSCIOUS

When a person/child is passed out or fainted. Call 911.

V

VOMIT

Throw up, barf, puke.

W

WHEEZING

A horse whistling sound that signals a breathing problem.

OPEN BOOK TEST

Babysitting Club

Date: _____

1. What age are babies?
2. What age are preschoolers?
3. What age are toddlers?
4. What age are school-aged children?
5. Should you ever shake a baby? YesNo
6. What is the universal emergency phone number?

   _____

7. Should you put a baby on their face to sleep?YesNo
8. It is important to follow the parents' rules and routine.Yes No
9. List **3** qualities of an excellent babysitter:

_____

_____

_____

_____

_____

_____

_____

_____

10. List **3** questions to ask during a telephone interview:

_____

_____

_____

_____

_____

_____

_____

_____

11. List **3** ways to prevent emergencies:

_____

_____

_____

_____

_____

_____

_____

_____

12. What do you do when a child has a nosebleed?

13. List **3** healthy snacks for **babies**:

_____

_____

_____

_____

_____

_____

_____

_____

toddlers:

_____

_____

_____

_____

_____

_____

_____

_____

preschool:

_____

_____

_____

_____

_____

_____

_____

_____

school-aged:

_____

_____

_____

_____

_____

_____

_____

_____

_____

1. True or False:
2. **Choking**: should you call 911 T F
3. **Poison**: if you suspect poisoning call 911 T F
4. **Seizure**: should you call 911 T F
5. **A Cold**: should you call 911 T F

15. DEFINITIONS

Airway: _____

Dispatcher: _____

Epi-Pen: _____

First Aid Kit: _____

Quiet Time: _____

Hygiene: _____

Moral Compass: _____

Resume: _____

16. What would you do if the child you are babysitting falls off a play gym at the park and is crying, holding their arm?

_____

_____

_____

_____

_____

_____

_____

_____

_____

16. (ii) What are some fun activities to do with a five-year old?

_____

_____

_____

_____

_____

_____

_____

_____

_____

16. (iii) What items are in a first aid kit?

_____

_____

_____

_____

_____

_____

_____

_____

16. (iv) What do you do if a stranger knocks on the door?

_____

_____

_____

_____

_____

_____

_____

_____

_____

16. (v) What should you do if the parents arrive home and what to drive you home, but you suspect they have been drinking too much?

_____

_____

_____

_____

_____

_____

_____

_____

16. (vi) What did you learn about babysitting?

_____

_____

_____

_____

_____

_____

_____

_____

Do you have any questions?

_____

_____

_____

_____

_____

_____

_____

I would like to add a bonus "Tips Section Here"

CITATIONS

The Canadian Red Cross. Babysitters Manual. Guelph, Ontario, The Stay Well Health Company Ltd. 2011

Copyright 2011 The Canadian Red Cross Society

The Canadian Red Cross. First Aid & CPR Manual. Guelph, Ontario, The Stay Well Health Company Ltd. 2011

These are the books and websites used for the research:

- Feeding For the First Year-
  https://www.stanfordchildrens.org/en/topic/default
  ?id=feeding-guide-for-the-first-year-90-P02209
- Sleeping For Children-
  https://www.sleepfoundation.org/excessive-
  sleepiness/support/how-much-sleep-do-babies-
  and-kids-need

- How to Hold a new Born Baby-
  https://www.healthline.com/health/parenting/how-to-hold-a-newborn
- Language Development Milestones kids age 1-4 years - https://www.parents.com/toddlers-preschoolers/development/language/language-development-milestones-ages-1-to-4/
- Safety Tips for Caregivers and Babysitters-
  https://www.kidpower.org/library/article/kidpower-safety-tips-for-babysitters-and-caregivers/
- Essential Babysitter First Aid And Safety Skills-
  https://www.kidpower.org/library/article/kidpower-safety-tips-for-babysitters-and-caregivers/
- How to be a good babysitter, Healthline Parenthood-
  https://www.healthline.com/health/parenting/how-to-be-a-good-babysitter

Made in United States
Troutdale, OR
12/19/2024